One Blood

Healing the Nation Divided

Earl Paulk

Destiny Image® Publishers, Inc.
P.O. Box 310
Shippensburg, PA 17257-0310

"Speaking to the Purposes of God for This Generation
and for the Generations to Come"

ISBN 1-56043-175-X

For Worldwide Distribution
Printed in the U.S.A.

Destiny Image books are available through these fine distributors outside the United States:

Christian Growth, Inc.
Jalan Kilang-Timor, Singapore 0315

Omega Distributors
Ponsonby, Auckland, New Zealand

Rhema Ministries Trading
Randburg, Rep. of South Africa

Salvation Book Centre
Petaling, Jaya, Malaysia

Successful Christian Living
Capetown, Rep. of South Africa

Vine Christian Centre
Mid Glamorgan, Wales, United Kingdom

WA Buchanan Company
Geebung, Queensland, Australia

Word Alive
Niverville, Manitoba, Canada

This book and all other Destiny Image and Treasure House books
are available at Christian bookstores everywhere.

Call for a bookstore nearest you.
1-800-722-6774
Or reach us on the Internet: **http://www.reapernet.com**

The late Jean Childs Young, wife of U.N. Ambassador Andrew Young, was recognized around the world for her tireless work as an educator, lecturer, civil and human rights activist, and community volunteer. She had strong concerns for national and international issues, particularly as they related to women and children. Bishop Earl Paulk has dedicated *One Blood* to this outstanding mother of four and grandmother of four children. Mrs. Young went home to be with the Lord in 1994.

Dedication

We dedicate this book, *One Blood*, to Jean Childs Young, late wife of Ambassador Andrew Young. In 1994, Mrs. Young went home to be with the Lord. She is greatly missed by her husband and her family, and all those who knew her.

Jean Young was noted not only for her work alongside her husband, but also in her own right as an educator, lecturer, civil and human rights activist, and community volunteer with strong concerns for national and international issues, particularly as they relate to women and children. She was the mother of four and a grandmother of four.

Total involvement and broad interests were hallmarks of the life of Jean Young as she successfully balanced her career, her family, and her participation, as a partner, in her husband's various career endeavors.

Jean and Andrew Young were key members of the team that successfully won the 1996 Olympics for Atlanta as they visited European, African, and Middle Eastern countries to solicit the votes of International Olympic Committee members.

As an educator, Mrs. Young served as a classroom teacher in Hartford, Connecticut, and Thomasville and Atlanta, Georgia; as coordinator of elementary and preschool programs with the Atlanta public school system; and as Lead Teacher in the Teacher Corps. She also participated in the development of Atlanta Metropolitan College and served as its Public Relations Officer and Instructor.

In her capacity as a community volunteer, Mrs. Young was founder, and served for seven years as chairperson, of the Mayor's Task Force on

Public Education—a group of Atlantans from all walks of life who are committed to improving the quality of education in Atlanta's public schools. This group sponsored the "Dream Jamboree," a career event that involved 15,000 high school students with representatives from colleges, universities, and other institutions, including private industry, that offer training or educational opportunities.

Mrs. Young lectured at local schools, churches, and civic and political organizations, and participated in fund-raising, publicity, and support for a wide range of programs. These programs include the activities of the United Negro College Fund, the Georgia Council on Child Abuse, the King Center, and First Congregational United Church of Christ.

In addition, Mrs. Young was the co-founder and co-chair of the Atlanta-Fulton County Commission on Children and Youth. She was chair of the Board of Directors for AOEX Museum and served on the Board of the Georgia Alliance for Public Education and the Board of "Sci Trek," the Science and Technology Museum of Atlanta. She was on the advisory boards of Outward Bound, SMART (Science, Math & Related Technologies), a program of the Girls Club, UNICEF, African American Studies Curriculum, and Habitat for Humanity.

As a Civil Rights Movement activist, Mrs. Young was intimately involved in numerous demonstrations and marches for human rights, including the 1963 March on Washington, the march from Selma to Montgomery in 1965, the Mississippi March in 1966, and the Poor People's Campaign in 1968.

Mrs. Young grew up in a small southern town—Marion, Alabama. She attended Manchester College in Indiana, where she received her B.S. degree in elementary education, and served as a member of the Board of Trustees of the college. She earned her M.S. degree in education from Queens College, New York, and continued graduate studies in education at the University of Georgia. She received honorary doctorates from Loyola University in Chicago and Manchester College, her alma mater.

On June 28, 1978, President Jimmy Carter appointed Jean Childs Young as chairperson of the United States National Commission of the International Year of the Child, a program under the auspices of the United Nations that is designed to improve the conditions of children throughout the world.

As wife and partner of Andrew Young, Mrs. Young was actively involved in her husband's work as pastor, civil rights leader, Congressman, United States Ambassador to the United Nations, Mayor of Atlanta, and then as an International business executive and co-chairman of the Atlanta Committee for the Olympic Games. Jean and Andrew Young had four children: Andrea, an attorney; Lisa, an electrical engineer; Paula, a preschool teacher, and Andrew III, a student at Florida A&M University, and are the grandparents of Taylor Marie Stanley, Kemet Louis Douglas Alston, Lena Marion Clarise Alston, and Caleb Wesley Young Shelton.

Acknowledgments

May I express my gratitude and indebtedness to several people who assisted me in writing this book.

First, my secretary Dottie Bridges, who went far beyond her job description, and spent days helping me.

My sister-in-law, Clariece Paulk, added much insight to the book and even added some of her own input to the text. She also provided the photographs.

Pastor James Powers was of untold value in his appraisal and addition to this effort.

Pastor Dan Rhodes added the scriptural reference that is very important to this message.

I am also indebted to a staff and church who have patiently listened to me across the years and lived out the demonstration that this book preaches.

Contents

Foreword

I have read with interest the book, *One Blood*, by Bishop Earl Paulk. Over the years I have respected this man of God, and his concern for all people. This book recounts some of his own personal life and also some of the history of the racial tension in Atlanta many years ago.

A couple of years ago, I was asked to be the keynote speaker at the fiftieth anniversary of Bishop Paulk's ministry. His church, I believe, is one that touches every aspect of life where there is a need. Luke 4:18-19 states, "The Spirit of the Lord is upon Me, because He hath anointed Me to preach the gospel to the poor; He hath sent Me to heal the brokenhearted, to preach deliverance to the captives, and recovering of sight to the blind, to set at liberty them that are bruised, to preach the acceptable year of the Lord." Chapel Hill Harvester Church has an Overcomers Ministry, which deals with all those who are addicted in every area; literacy programs; scouting programs; and art programs—and they have taken their programs into some of Atlanta's most crime-infested public housing communities.

As a young boy Bishop Paulk began to notice the racial bigotry and determined to do something about it. All his life he has taught and demonstrated racial harmony. His church now demonstrates that all races can live and worship together in unity.

I am honored that Bishop Paulk has dedicated this book to my late wife, Jean. Bishop Paulk was able to minister to her during the last few weeks of her life. We are grateful for his care.

Andrew Young
Atlanta, Georgia
May, 1996

Chapter 1

"I'll Make This
Up to You, Sammy"

I stepped away from the door of the church in the fall of 1948 and felt a cold chill run down my spine. It was only my second Sunday as the pastor of a small church in Buford, Georgia. I was 21 years old when I walked out to face the crowd of white-hooded Ku Klux Klan members parading in front of the church that morning. The fear didn't matter. I had made up my mind long before the hooded racists showed up at the front door of the church.

I knew I would stir up a hornet's nest that first Sunday morning, because I preached a controversial sermon to my new congregation on the ills of racial problems. I even dared to teach that the Bible says Christ died for all men—regardless of color. It was my opinion (although unpopular at the time) that the laws of God in the Bible were higher than any Jim Crow laws written in the law books of the State of Georgia to "keep colored people in their place."

Obviously several members of my first church congregation were members of the Ku Klux Klan, because the very next Sunday, our church service was interrupted by the raucous sound of blowing horns. Somebody in the church suddenly announced, "The Ku Klux Klan is out here!" and I left the service and stepped outside to confront the hooded men parading in front of the church on that beautiful Sunday morning.

Amid the shouts, threats, and obscenities leveled at me that day, I somehow recognized the voice of one of my own parishioners! I later learned that a number of the men in my congregation were active members

1

of the Klan. The man whose voice I identified that day later admitted to me that he was in the Klan parade. He said, "Pastor, you didn't have to worry. I wasn't going to let those boys hurt you. That was just a warning to you to soft-pedal this business about the race situation."

My confrontation with the Klan on my second Sunday as a pastor marked the beginning of a battle I would fight all my life. It was here that the first of many people challenged me to my face with what became a familiar statement: "We don't want you here in this church to preach to us if you're a nigger-lover!"

Nearly a decade earlier, I had stood in a water shed crying, "Sammy, oh no...Sammy!" as I watched the blood trickle down the dust-stained black skin of my friend's back. Tears were running down his cheeks, and I'll never forget the look of fear in his eyes. "Oh, Sammy, I'm sorry! I promise...as God is my witness...I'll make this up to you someday!"

Every summer, Mama and Daddy used to take me to the farm to stay with my grandmother and granddaddy. Sometimes I stayed with my uncles and aunts. Now, one of my uncles had a bad temper, and whenever he got mad, he had a habit of acting very quickly without thinking.

That particular day, he had instructed Sammy, "Now boy, you be sure you go all the way to the end of the row with the plow, and don't cut off the corners. That just plows up good cotton." But Sammy was tired and hot, and he forgot.

Now I'm sure my uncle had no thought of killing Sammy. Afterward, he told us, "After all, it was just bird shot—everybody knows that can't seriously injure a person. But the boy needed to learn a lesson!"

When I reached my friend, Sammy was in pain; but the pain in his back was not nearly as severe as the pain in his heart. I thought my own heart was going to burst as I took him to the water shed and grabbed a towel. I started to very gently wash the blood from Sammy's perforated back, while wondering, *Why? Why? Sammy was my friend!* I didn't care about his skin color. He was defenseless, and he had been taken advantage of. All I could say at that time was, "...I'll make this up to you someday." Little did I realize what I was saying.

My daddy was a Pentecostal preacher, and for him, summertime meant attending camp meetings all over the United States. To me, it meant spending my summer days on the farm. (Now that was really "heaven" to this city boy.) But after the incident with Sammy, I didn't know what to think about farm life anymore.

The shooting of Sammy in southern Georgia's Appling County was not my first encounter with "the race problem." The first question in my mind about racial differences arose in Logan, West Virginia, where my dad was pastoring a church early in my childhood. We lived in the church parsonage, next door to a black family that had a little girl who was just about my age. I thought she was the most beautiful person I had ever seen. (I certainly didn't think that we were "different.")

One day she was playing in her yard, and I could resist no longer. I went over to the fence and asked her to come over and talk to me. Then I hugged her right there through the fence. At that very moment, my mother looked out and saw what was happening. Horrified, she called for me to come into the house immediately. Then she "explained the way more perfectly." For the first time, I heard what I would hear again and again as I grew up in Georgia: "It's okay to love colored people, as long as they stay in their place." I still couldn't imagine why my mother was so upset with me. I only hugged my little friend. What was the problem? Throughout my life, this "problem" raised its ugly head again and again.

Summer came again, but that year I visited another uncle who took me in his truck to a place he called "shantytown." I had never been there before, and I had no idea what it would be like. Later on, I heard people describe "shantytown" as "the place where the darkies live." (At that time, I had never heard the phrase, "African-American.")

Shantytown turned out to be a great disappointment to me. It was just horrible. I really can't describe the shacks in which these people lived. There were no indoor toilets, nor was there any running water. (The whole community shared one well.) The white farmers in the area also had outdoor toilets, but they were very nice. And every white family had its own well, with an adequate supply of water for them, their cattle, and other animals.

The "houses" these black people lived in were not really houses at all; they were called "lean-tos." (I guess if you leaned on them, they would fall over. Or perhaps they got that name because they all seemed to lean to one side or the other.) Anyway, an indelible impression was printed on my mind that day: Something was terribly wrong for there to be so much difference between the quality of life for two races of people living side by side.

In defense of my parents, I must say that I was never allowed to call these people "nigger." I would have been harshly corrected if I had used that term. I was taught to say the polite term in vogue in those days: "colored folk." I was never quite sure where "their place" was, and I really thought about it, because I was always hearing white people say of colored people, "They're okay—in their own place." Where was their place? It was quite evident to me that their place was a long distance from white people.

This uncle's farmhouse didn't have electric lights, so we spent our nights entertaining ourselves by telling stories around a gas lamp or lantern. One particular story about my grandfather really upset me. The tale was that one night my grandfather fired a shot in the general direction of a young black man. The next morning, it was learned that a young black man had been shot in that same area. We never knew for sure what actually happened, but when Grandpa lay on his deathbed, he desperately wanted to be sure that all his sins were confessed and forgiven.

I had heard of lynchings and other cruel slayings of black men, and I realized that something was wrong when there seemed to be such a lack of appreciation for human life when it was housed in a black body. Some of the other stories that upset me were about white men wearing white hoods who flogged and killed black men for supposedly neglecting their families. I couldn't figure it out: I knew some white men who didn't care for their families either. In fact, we regularly delivered food and clothing to their homes, but they were never visited or punished by the mysterious men in the ominous white hoods. Why?

I also learned that the hooded men punished black men for "getting out of their place." That meant they should never dare to speak to a white woman about anything. White women, for their part, were sternly instructed to keep their distance from black men, because "danger was involved." I noticed that any time a white woman was raped or assaulted, you could be sure a black man would be punished (guilty or not).

While all this was going on, I also began to hear teenage white boys openly laughing about their sexual activities with young black women.

I just couldn't understand the community's lack of concern about this problem. Something was definitely wrong.

Ironically, certain black people were really accepted, especially those who worked in the homes of white families, doing the cooking, ironing, cleaning, and any other jobs they were asked to do. Ruth was a gracious and beautiful "colored" lady who worked in our family home in Greenville, South Carolina. She was literally accepted as a member of our family, and we loved her very dearly. In fact, my parents sternly taught us to give Ruth our total respect and obedience!

We went to church twice every Sunday, and many nights during the week. The only black person we ever saw at the church was the janitor. Now he didn't really attend the services, but he was always around the church working, cleaning, and repairing whatever was broken. We were expected to respect him as well. Occasionally, a black choir would visit the church, but it was always made clear that this was "just a visit" and there would be no regular practice of worshiping together with "colored" people.

My dad's church in Greenville was one of the largest Pentecostal churches in the nation at that time. Naturally, we had a lot of guests come through our doors. It was even considered acceptable for artists of other races to visit—especially if they sang as well as one young man who was called out of the audience to sing one day. We had no idea how famous he would become, but as it happened, the young "colored" singer was none other than Nat King Cole.

My father was really a wonderful man, but he was a product of the environment in which he was raised. He was kind, and he wouldn't hurt a flea, but he had been taught that some things were "just a way of life." I can still remember him preaching about the need to send missionaries to Africa. He would literally cry as he shared the accounts of missionaries who had been sent to villages on the "dark continent" to minister to the helpless natives there. Every time, the congregation would cry as well, and come down the aisles with their offerings to send another missionary to Africa.

The man my father and other ministers lifted up as a saint in those days was "Brother Stark," a missionary who had died in Africa while ministering to the people. I just couldn't put the pieces together. I knew firsthand that the black people at home had needs just like the black people in Africa, but "God forbid that we take an offering for them or try to improve the quality of their lives in any way." What could I do? I was just a young boy, yet something had to be done.

Whenever I asked a question about this contradiction in any sort of religious gathering, I never really got an answer, and I was usually told to be quiet. Yet I pondered these questions in my heart, and I vowed before God that when I was grown, somehow I would do something (although I had no idea what I could do).

Due to the strict rules of our denomination, I wasn't allowed to attend movies or very many athletic events, and we usually ate at home. But whenever I went to a service station or the railroad station, and when we occasionally ate a meal at a restaurant, I noticed the signs posted over every bathroom and water fountain that said, "White Only" and "Colored." Most of the time, rest rooms were reserved for whites only, and no provision was made for black people. How unfair. I think my generation just assumed that these decisions were not within our grasp—they were to be handled "by our elders." We waited for our elders to make some statement, but the statement never came. You didn't have to be an attorney to see that some of the state's written Jim Crow laws were absolutely contradictory to the Constitution of the United States, yet the status quo continued to rule the day without challenge.

I am a student of history. How else can we know how to avoid mistakes today if we don't study the past? I believe that "how you view is what you do." A great conviction must take root in the inner man before any action is taken. Once an inner conviction pounds loudly enough in our brains and our hearts, then we cannot sit still and do nothing. I instinctively knew that the day would come when my uneasy feelings would explode and be transformed into action.

I used to listen to preachers in the 1940's and 50's try to justify their stand on racism from behind a pulpit and on radio. Frankly, I never heard any one of them put up a good argument. Most of them referred vaguely to the Israelites, "…who were told not to marry among pagan nations." In my mind, God was dealing with Israel through the prophets when He warned them not to be joined to pagan gods. That had nothing to do with racial integration.

The Bible makes it clear that Moses was married to a woman who was not of his race, and when Aaron and Miriam became upset and accused him, they were severely punished by God.[1] Yet most pulpits across the nation, and particularly throughout the South, said nothing. It was as if the race issue did not even exist. "Don't talk about it, and it'll go away." Unfortunately, the Church could not take a stand because it was too involved with the dominant political and economic forces of the South. None of this made sense to me.

My conviction was that we were all of one race originally. We were only separated into different races and language groups because of our disobedience and rebellion. Because of our pride and stubborn desire to "do it our way" at the Tower of Babel, our tongues (or languages) were confused, and this was not corrected until the Day of Pentecost.

The distinguishing mark of the Day of Pentecost was that all races were brought together in one accord.[2] What happened to the unity of the early Church? How did we ever get into such a mess in America? I was about to explode. I prayed, "God, give me an opportunity to make a difference!" The time was not far away.

---

1. Numbers 12:1-15.
2. Acts 2:8-11.

Chapter 2

The Rising Storm

A wonderful thing happened during my last year of college at Furman University in Greenville, South Carolina. I married Norma Davis, whom I had known since she was a little girl in my father's church in Greenville. She became a vital part of my ministry, and after we graduated from Furman University, we worked together in Sunday school and youth leadership in Georgia.

As fall approached, I received a phone call asking me to come to Lee College in Cleveland, Tennessee. I knew I was called to be a pastor, and I did not want to teach in college, but when the elders of my father's church denomination asked you to do something, you did it. Very reluctantly, Norma and I moved to Tennessee, knowing it would be an interim position. I was frustrated most of the time, and my only relief came when I was able to preach on weekends.

After we had spent a year serving at Lee College, I was given a scholarship to attend the Candler School of Theology at Emory University in Atlanta. I was appointed to fill in for pastors and care for two small charges during the summer, and when fall arrived, I was assigned to the pastorate in Buford, Georgia, just north of Atlanta. I also enrolled at Emory University and became a student of theology (in between encounters with the Ku Klux Klan and unhappy parishioners).

Living in Georgia was a new experience for me. Although I had been born in Appling County, I had never lived in Georgia, except for one year when our family moved to Macon. Coming back to Georgia did not feel much like coming home. I had lived all over the East Coast, and sometimes I attended two different schools in the same year.

Little did I know that God had joined me to this city, and to a great cause that would be birthed here. Atlanta, at that time, was home to approximately 300,000 people, plus a few thousand more who lived in the metropolitan area.

I had not been in the area long before I sensed a tension in the city—racial tension. There was a deep restlessness stirring among black men and women, and not just in Atlanta. It permeated the South. I heard about Auburn Avenue and some of the financial gains in the black community, and realized that power was beginning to move into the black community in Atlanta.

Meanwhile, we continued to minister at the church in Buford, where I taught the children how to sing that remarkable song, "Jesus loves the little children, all the children of the world...red and yellow, black and white, they are precious in His sight..." I could see the bitterness in the expressions of the elders and the adults in the congregation, but the kids received the truth of the song with joy. I realized then that the kids were where the victory was going to be—we had to bring them up free of prejudice.

In 1951, I graduated from Candler School of Theology and was appointed as pastor of an old-line Pentecostal church in Atlanta, the Hemphill Avenue Church of God (now the Mt. Paran Church of God). When I took the pastorate, I discovered that the leadership of the church was very closely tied to local and state government officials.

Government officials in that day generally believed that segregation was the only proper social structure for the South. The Talmadge family dominated politics from the governor's mansion in Georgia for nearly two generations, and particularly at the time I moved to Atlanta to pastor the Hemphill Avenue Church of God church.

One of the elders at the Hemphill Avenue church used to bake a cake for the Talmadge family every year. Any time we wanted the governor to speak at our denomination's camp meetings or services, this elder would call up the Talmadges on the phone and the governor would show up to speak. As you can imagine, the leadership of the local church was not very happy when I began to speak out against racial prejudice and social injustice.

I certainly do not fault this elder, or any of the other local church leaders, because this was their background. They were very sincere men, and they believed deeply in their convictions (although that didn't make them right). There had been no teaching concerning God's plan of equality for all men.[1]

I became even more unpopular when I joined the Atlanta Christian Council. The Council was a powerful force in those days. This coalition of between 300 and 400 Atlanta churches was the elite religious group in the city. Any opinion or recommendation it issued carried great weight with political leaders and communities.

Ralph Byrd, the pastor of Faith Memorial Assembly of God, was one of my mentors at the time. He went to the Christian Council with me just to accompany me, really, and we both wound up on the executive committee because we were the only Pentecostal representatives there! The Atlanta Christian Council wanted to have representatives from each denomination, and the heads of each group sat on the executive committee. Brother Byrd represented the Assemblies, and I sat in for the Church of God.

Pastor Byrd had ministered in Africa, in the Philippines, and in many other places, and he had experienced such marvelous miracles in his ministry that any prejudice he might have had previously was completely broken down. Both Pastor Byrd and I were very comfortable with the Atlanta Christian Council, which spoke out concerning controversial issues of the day.

The conservative Christian community generally considered members of the Christian Council to be liberal in their thinking. Most of these pastors not only avoided the Christian Council, but many times, actively opposed it and preached against it. They felt it was tied to the World Council of Churches, which they also opposed. They judged the members of the Christian Council to be unfit because some of the members of the Council smoked cigarettes, a practice they strongly preached against.

Those were the days of Atlanta's famous preachers. My colleagues on the Atlanta Christian Council included the great Peter Marshall, who was later called to be the Chaplain of the U.S. Senate; and Charles Allen from Grace Methodist (who would later pastor the largest Methodist church in America). There was also the pastor of First Methodist Church, the well-known Dr. Pierce Harris, and the popular pastor of the First Baptist Church

---

1.   See Romans 10:12; Galatians 3:28; Colossians 3:11.

of Atlanta, Roy McClain. The president of the Atlanta Christian Council at that time was Dr. James Wesberry, the pastor of Morningside Baptist Church. All these were great men who were dealing with the racial problem in their own churches at the time.

The Civil Rights Movement had begun to surface by the early 1950's. There had been some nonviolent "sit-ins" at lunch counters by defiant blacks, and then in Alabama, a young black woman named Rosa Parks refused to move to the back of the bus in defiance of the Jim Crow laws of that state. This was the incident that was "heard around the world," and unofficially marked the birth of the American Civil Rights Movement.

Through my association with the Atlanta Christian Council, I heard about a group of men who were meeting in the basement of the Ebenezer Baptist Church on Auburn Avenue to discuss the racial situation. The son of the pastor there was beginning to win a reputation for his daring sermons against the evils of segregation and his strong message of non-violent protest. I wanted to hear more.

I decided to take a risk and attend the meeting at Ebenezer Baptist. I went on my own, not as a representative of the Atlanta Christian Council. I drove across the "line" at Buttermilk Bottom into the "colored" section of Atlanta and walked into the basement of the church, knowing I had crossed another line from which there would be no return.

When I walked through the door that day, I saw Martin Luther King, Jr., sitting on the side of a table, just like any other young fellow having a good time. The young men around him were kidding him about something, and they were all laughing. I walked in right in the middle of this, and it was obvious to me that they were concerned when they saw a young white man walk into the building. I knew they wondered why I had come.

Someone came up to me right away and asked me what I was doing there, and I said, "Oh, I came to the meeting tonight. I'm the pastor of the Hemphill Avenue Church of God church." This person had heard about the church, and I could tell he was surprised. Soon after that, a lady came to me and led me over to Martin Luther King, Jr., to introduce me. She said, "This man is a pastor from a Church of God here in the city, and he wants to come to the meeting today."

Martin Luther Jr. looked at me and grasped my hand in both of his hands and said, "I just appreciate your coming. It will take people like you and me to make a difference." He couldn't have given me a warmer reception. The impact of Martin Luther Jr.'s remark stuck in my mind permanently. I realized I was running a terrible risk with my church and the city by coming to the meeting that day. Associating with those men in the basement of Ebenezer Baptist Church was not a widely accepted thing in those days, not even among black ministers. That meeting took place in the fall of 1951, or the spring of 1952. I was about 25 or 26 years old, and Martin Luther King, Jr., was two years younger than I was.

The men who gathered in the basement of Ebenezer Baptist came to be known as the "Concerned Clergy," and though the purpose of the group took on different natures as the years went on, the primary purpose of its members was to hear the cry of the various ethnic groups and be concerned enough about the issues to "put their name on the line" for their convictions. (As I recall, only three or four white men ever became a part of the Concerned Clergy in those years, and at the time, the only other white clergyman to join the group was an Episcopal priest.) Most black pastors stayed away from the meetings too, in response to threats of violence if they came to those sessions.

I sat in on the meeting on that particular night as the sole white representative. Daddy King moderated the meeting that night, and Martin Luther King, Jr., didn't play a leading role. I guess Daddy King wanted to see if I was scared, because he began the meeting by looking directly at me and saying, "You boys ready to go to jail for this thing?" (In those days, you would be put in jail if you broke any of the Jim Crow laws of Georgia. As I mentioned before, Georgia laws were different from the national laws.) Everyone in the room said, "We are ready if necessary."

After that, Martin Luther King, Jr., gave a report about a nonviolent protest march he was trying to organize in Alabama after the Rosa Parks incident. It looked like it was finally going to take place, and some of the men in the meeting that night were supposed to go over there and help him with it. The march had been strategized by the group before I became involved, but I was one of the brethren who gave final approval and support for that first civil rights march, knowing we would have to stay with it once the fire was lit.

When a controversial U.S. Supreme Court ruling was handed down requiring state governments to provide equal education for all citizens regardless of race or color, the government of the State of Georgia decided to follow the lead of Governor Wallace in Alabama, who defied Federal troops and physically blocked the doors of a school to prevent integration.

Georgia officials said it would be better to close the state's public schools than integrate them. That is when I decided to speak out in my own pulpit and preached my boldest message to date, urging the congregation to see that the schools remain open and that we love all people, regardless of the color of their skin. This sermon did not seal my fate, but my next action would.

The church elders approached me after the service and told me I had ruined their political situation with the Talmadge family, but I knew I hadn't really hurt them. I knew Herman Talmadge better than any of the elders did, and my daddy knew him even better than I did. The truth was that although Herman Talmadge appeared to be a very racist man on the surface, down in his heart it made no difference. He really didn't care. I knew the racist image of the Talmadge family was just for political expediency.

Several members of the Christian Council, and particularly those of us on the executive committee, began to draft a manifesto declaring that the schools should remain open and should be integrated according to the Federal laws. When this manifesto was printed on the front pages of the *Atlanta Journal* and the *Atlanta Constitution*, everyone was especially eager to find out who had signed the covenant. Of course my name, along with that of Brother Ralph Byrd, was included in the list, since we had helped to frame the statement.

(Only 80 members of the Atlanta Christian Council signed the first "Atlanta Manifesto." Twelve months later, a second statement on "The South's Racial Crisis" was issued by the Council and signed by 312 ministers and rabbis from Greater Atlanta.)

The "Atlanta Manifesto" instantly became a point of controversy among the Atlanta churches, and several pastors resigned or were sent to other parishes during that period of time.

The Federal government gradually began to respond to changing public opinion across the country by pressuring state governments and segregated school districts in the South to integrate their schools. At first, Georgia officials threatened to close the schools rather than submit to integration of any sort. That prompted a flood of negative reactions (and inspired my "politically incorrect" sermon), so state officials reluctantly retreated to a backup strategy by claiming that Georgia's public schools could satisfy these demands by remaining "separate but equal."

The Atlanta Christian Council was skeptical of this claim, but the Georgia State Senate and House of Representatives hoped to win us over. The Council appointed me and four other people (including members of the executive committee and two legislators) to a committee to observe schools all over the state. Our task was to determine if the schools were indeed "separate but equal." The state legislature was hoping we would bring back a report that would say, "Yes, the schools are separate, but there is equal opportunity in both the black and the white communities regarding public education."

This just was not the case, however. I went into some small towns in South Georgia where modern new grammar schools and high schools had been built for white children. Just a few yards away stood the "equal" school facility for black children. Five grades were crammed into one classroom. A lone pot-bellied stove at the front of the room was supposed to provide heat for the classroom, but the children were shivering in the cold. The walls were not painted, and there was no running water or inside toilets. This wasn't equality. To a man, our committee came back saying it was ridiculous. I began to cry out that there was absolutely no such thing as "separate but equal."

Meanwhile, the tension in Atlanta rose higher and higher, and many acts of violence were taking place. Something had to be done. It was during this time that the mayor of Atlanta began to call on members of the Atlanta Christian Council and the Concerned Clergy to serve as negotiators between the extremist groups. The two men who served as mayor during the most turbulent years were Mayor Hartsfield and Mayor Ivan Allen. Both of these men were very broad-minded, and they genuinely wanted to have peace in our city. I remember spending many evenings trying to reconcile the problems of our city along with Martin Luther King, Jr., Daddy King, and many of the other leaders across the city. It had become very dangerous to be in public places at night.

With all the violence going on, I was constantly being called to make emergency visits to area hospitals. With tension running so high in those days, these visits across town really posed some danger. I decided to begin wearing a clerical collar to let people know that I was doing the ministry of the Church. At the time, it was something that served a specific purpose, but later on, I wore a clerical collar out of a conviction that God placed on my heart.

My father and I had been very good friends with both Eugene and Herman Talmadge, and of course they were caught in the midst of the battle that was raging throughout Georgia. Strangely enough, the nearest business establishment to the church I pastored then was the Pickrick Restaurant. Its owner, Lester Maddox, was soon to become governor.

Lester ran a paid column in the newspaper every week in which he spewed out pure racist dogma. His campaign was so popular among certain groups that he was soon propelled to the office of governor primarily on the basis of his racist views! He became known by the media and the citizens of Georgia as "the man who encouraged the symbol of ax handles to stop integration." Lester Maddox distributed thousands of free ax handles from his restaurant only a few yards from the front door of the church I pastored. He publicly urged people to stop integration at the voting booths, restaurants, or any other place they saw "integration" taking place (despite the fact that Federal law already guaranteed equal access to these places for all U.S. citizens, regardless of color or race).

I had many conversations with Lester Maddox over a cup of coffee in his restaurant. I liked Lester, and he made it clear that he liked and respected me as well, but he thought I was "far too liberal." Most of his comments to me were limited to statements like, "Hi there, Pastor. I heard your radio show today—I really liked that song." Sometimes I would jokingly say, "Lester, I'm praying for you that you'll get saved." (He was a member of the Baptist church.) Yet I knew what was brewing under the surface, and many times I left his place knowing the State of Georgia was headed into some dark days. It was as if I could see "the handwriting on the wall." Only God could help us. I began calling the church to prayer because I knew there was going to be much bloodshed if something was not done. (Lester Maddox is still alive and living in Atlanta at this writing.)

By the end of the 1950's, things had really gotten out of hand and many violent confrontations were taking place. After I signed the "Atlanta

Manifesto," relationships with certain members of the local church leadership became even more strained, and I was convinced that I had to make a change. Although I desperately loved the people at Hemphill Avenue Church of God, I resigned as pastor (and as a member of the denomination) and left with a heavy heart after serving there for eight years.

Only weeks before that, I had received a unanimous vote of affirmation from the congregation, but I knew that God was calling me to something new (though I couldn't have expressed it at that time). This change was especially difficult because this was my family's denomination. In fact, my father was the assistant general overseer of the area for the national organization. Yet I had to follow the leading of the Holy Spirit as best I could.

When I left Atlanta, the Lord really spoke to my brother-in-law, Harry Mushegan, and my sister, Myrtle, that we should go together. My younger brother, Don, also felt led to go with us. Harry pastored a church in Daisy, Tennessee, and he was just as unhappy with some of the church denomination's regulations as I was, but he didn't know a way out. After much prayer, Harry felt it was absolutely necessary to stay with me. We all loaded up our kids, and Don joined us for a road trip out West.

We didn't know we would stop in Phoenix, Arizona, but we decided to spend some time with Harry's brother, who pastored a church there. When he asked us to hold a revival in the church, we agreed and quickly discovered that the thing wouldn't stop! This revival went on for six weeks, and people were being saved all over the place. The superintendent's wife received the baptism in the Holy Ghost, and another man who owned property there offered to give us printing presses and a school if we stayed there.

During the three months we spent in Phoenix, I was dealing with an unbelievable sense of personal grief over the flock I had left in Atlanta. I had fasted for three or four days at one point, and was praying for a clear direction from the Lord. At the time I had decided to start an evangelistic association to deal primarily with college campuses. As the first "Pentecostal-born" graduate of a "legitimate" seminary, I wanted to reach out to the educational world. Yet something was missing from the picture.

One morning, as I lay prostrate on my face before the Lord, Brother Mushegan came into the bedroom after Norma had left to go to breakfast. He physically picked me up off the floor and said, "Earl, that's enough."

Within the next few weeks, I heard the Lord really speak to me about returning to Atlanta. Brother Mushegan was my brother-in-law, but he was more than that—he was like a spiritual father to me in a lot of ways. He is still an important man in my life. He pastors a great church across town, and we are still associated together.

The Lord spoke to us that we were to return to Atlanta to "nothin'." Just before we returned to Georgia, I went out to Los Angeles, California, and preached a revival in the Armenian church there attended by Demos Shakarian and his family.

It was clear that God had a plan for Atlanta, the jewel of the South that had been burned to the ground by General Sherman during the Civil War. Atlanta...this city had risen again from the ashes of destruction like the phoenix bird. Atlanta was called the "little New York of the South" and the city that was "too busy to hate."

We loaded our families and our few possessions into two cars pulling trailers and headed back to Atlanta early in 1960. My younger brother, Don, was about to be married, and his bride, Clariece, joined our team. Less than a century after the Civil War, we were planting a new work in the city that had just become the birthplace of the Civil Rights Movement, the home of America's most militant black racists, and the national headquarters of the Ku Klux Klan!

We planted the new church in a part of the city where there was no Pentecostal work, with a totally new group of people. We bought the old St. John's Lutheran Church building in Atlanta, which was situated near the "Little Five Points" area of Atlanta. It was the closest white church to Ebenezer Baptist Church, where the King family ministered. I had only been away from Atlanta for about three months, and I immediately began attending the Concerned Clergy meetings again. This time I was joined by my brother, Don.

As usual, Daddy King moderated most of the meetings, and he always began with his trademark challenge: "Now boys, are you ready to go to jail for your convictions?" Of course, we all accepted the challenge. We were trying to form a strategy to stop some of the violence in the city. Martin Luther King, Jr., was gone most of the time at that point, but he occasionally dropped by to speak to us about what was taking place around the country. More than ever, I realized that Daddy King was a man of great spiritual power, and a very powerful force behind his son.

Our church was located on Euclid Avenue, which was the dividing line between the black and white neighborhoods. Like many cities, a set of railroad tracks divided the area, so we had a "right side" of the tracks, and a so-called "wrong side" of the tracks. It was common knowledge that you just didn't cross the railroad tracks at night. Whites didn't dare go over into the "colored" section called "Buttermilk Bottom," and blacks didn't dare to cross over to the white community.

The "white side" had streets lined with beautiful old mansions, including the old Asa Candler (who had amassed the Coca-Cola fortune) home. Unfortunately, most of these homes had been nearly destroyed when the people who had moved out of the area decided to divide these structures into multi-family dwellings. Many poor or uneducated white people lived in them at the time, and many of the area's problems came from a colony of hippies that had moved into one of the houses right across the street from the church.

It was not a strange sight to see our neighbors fighting at all hours. Every night, they would get drunk on cheap peach wine and end up beating one another's heads into the pavement in public brawls. No black person dared to come near when the people across from the church were drinking; so of course, there were no blacks in the church.

My old friend, Lester Maddox, had already left the governor's office by the time we came to Euclid Avenue in 1960. I had waited a long time to see my dream come to pass, and I sensed that the time had come to press on with my idea to integrate our congregation. Our church was independent and free of the discrimination-prone church government structure so common in the South at that time. Now we pastored a church that was situated only two blocks away from the "dividing line" between Atlanta's white and black population. On the "other side of the tracks" stood Ebenezer Baptist Church. If I was going to follow through with my plan, then it was also time to really count the cost.

We declared our intentions with our very first church brochure, which featured a picture of a black hand and white hand clasped together in a handshake. Then I thought of a way to integrate the church without overly disturbing people in their communities. I felt it was too dangerous to bring a local black family "across the tracks" to our services, since they still had to live and function in their communities. The threat of violence was too great for local residents at that time.

One of the members of our congregation was Daniel Fugi, a Japanese student attending Atlanta University. One night over dinner I asked, "Fugi, do you have any black friends at the university?" He smiled and said, "Oh yes, I know some black students from Africa. They are attending the Inter-denominational Theological Center near Morris Brown College." Then I said, "I'd like you to get one or two carloads of your African friends and bring them to our church as guests."

I didn't tell anybody else about my plan, so none of the church people knew what was going to happen. At the appointed hour, just as the church service began, Daniel Fugi walked in the door with enough of his African friends to fill two full pews in the church sanctuary! I wondered what response our "integration effort" would get, and it didn't take long to find out. I watched as a dozen people immediately stood up and walked out the door, leaving about a hundred stunned people gaping in their seats.

One of the people who left was a deacon. He was a good man and an ex-police officer, but as he walked out of the building, he loudly muttered, "I'm not going to stay in this place with these people!" That is when a quiet little white lady stood up before another word could be said, and turned toward the silent congregation.

I had never heard Sister Ida Sanders say anything in public, except for a brief personal testimony. She was a quiet, timid woman who was always content to listen to other people talk. On that historic day in Georgia, she was a miracle. She began to speak, and her words hit us with incredible power and authority:

"That which God has called clean, how can you call unclean!"

I still remember how the veins stood out in her neck as she walked and prophesied to us by the Spirit of God. Sister Sanders was angry that morning, but her anger was a type of righteous indignation that was clearly from God. She only had a third-grade education, and she was not a public speaker. Of all the people in that church service that morning, she should have been a racist. She was born and raised as a poor and uneducated white woman in the South, and the state-approved racism helped maintain her "status" in southern society—but the Spirit of God had prepared her for "such a time as this."

All we could do was listen. There was no question that God was speaking with supernatural eloquence through this woman. Sister Sanders walked those aisles like an anointed tent preacher, and for a full quarter of an hour, preached a sermon that would live on in every heart that was there. She cried out, "It was not the will of God that we should have prejudices!" Many of the people in the congregation just sat and cried, either in repentance or anger. Meanwhile, those young African students hardly knew what was going on.

We realized that something had taken place in our church that could never be changed. There were lines drawn that morning that forced people to make decisions about their future. From that day on, there was no way to turn back and no place to run. I was glad to see some of the people who left the service that morning come back later, including the deacon. He apologized to me for leaving—he was too sold out to God to resist the Holy Spirit, even if it meant worshiping with "those people."

After Sister Sanders sat down, we sang a song or two and I began to preach. Then I was told that a mob had gathered outside, and they appeared to be waiting for everyone inside to come out of the church building. I turned the service over to Don and stepped outside to confront the mob (but the congregation didn't know why I went out).

The crowd wasn't an organized group. It was mostly composed of neighbors who had heard that "colored people" had gone into our church building. The word had quickly spread through the neighborhood that the church had black people in the service. Some of the kids probably saw the African students arrive, and ran to tell their parents. In those days, it was unusual to see black people go into a white church. Most of the people who lived on Druid Circle across from the church loved and respected us. We ministered to them in many ways, but they just couldn't handle the "race problem."

When I walked out to meet the people, I couldn't help but notice the homemade and makeshift weapons in their hands and the look in their eyes. I told them I was going to call the police and have them dispersed if they did not move away on their own. Then I challenged them to drop the weapons in their hands, because I knew what their intentions were. By the grace of God, the people in the crowd heard my cry. Evidently they were convinced that I meant business because, for the most part, they simply disappeared. When I was satisfied that the crisis was over, I went back into the service and resumed preaching the message God had given me for that day, and God visited with us.

At about the same time, Don and I went to Ebenezer Baptist for a Concerned Clergy meeting where we decided to challenge a produce market in Buttermilk Bottom. The white grocers who owned this market were going to the different farmer's markets at the Atlanta Municipal City Market and purchasing discarded and nearly spoiled produce and other foods.

They brought the stuff back to their Buttermilk Bottom market and hawked the "food" at exorbitant prices, thinking they could sell the nearly spoiled produce and food to the black residents in that area because they were a "captive market." Like many inner-city residents in public housing projects and depressed areas of large cities, these people were "trapped" because they had no transportation to travel beyond their neighborhood and shop in other areas.

When we investigated the problem, we learned, for instance, that a head of lettuce selling for 50 cents in an exclusive (and expensive) white Atlanta neighborhood like Buckhead was being marked up to 60 cents in Buttermilk Bottom (even though it was spoiled and virtually inedible). We felt that the abuse was so bad that something had to be done. We contacted the owners of the market and talked to them personally. When they refused to pay any attention to our claims or warnings, we decided to march on the market to make the community aware of the abuse.

We literally made placards and publicly picketed the market. The market operators apparently got the names of each of the protesters involved, because we received notice that a lawsuit was being filed against us for a million dollars. They did it just to scare us because it never went to court, and the market was shut down.

The threat of the lawsuit was still over our heads when Norma and I were invited to Detroit with Don and Clariece to preach in some services up there. We were driven off the road in that city by a carload of black men who were cursing us because we had a Georgia automobile license tag. I guess they assumed we had to be racists because we were from Georgia.

Those angry black men thought they were striking a blow for racial equality, but the four white people in the car they ran off the road that day were deeply involved in the battle to bring about proper racial harmony in Georgia. They cursed us for being white residents of Georgia, but we had literally put our lives on the line to try and bring about racial integration in an appropriate way. This incident simply shows that evil will arise in people of any race when prejudice runs rampant in the streets.

Then came one of the saddest days in the history of Atlanta, Georgia, and of the nation. Newscasters across the United States announced that Martin Luther King, Jr., had been assassinated in Memphis, Tennessee. We could not believe what we were hearing. We were pastoring the white church that was nearest to the black community, even within shouting distance of Ebenezer Baptist Church, where Dr. King's family attended.

Violence instantly erupted in the streets of Atlanta. Windows were broken, and angry people threw bottles everywhere. We had just moved to the nearby community of Decatur, Georgia, when I heard the news of Dr. King's death. I immediately called Don and Clariece at their home next door to the church and told them, "You'd better come out and spend the night with us."

When they returned to their home the following morning, the first person to knock on their door was an Orkin exterminator who happened to be a young black man. Clariece went to the door and said, "Come in. I want to tell you how sorry we are that your leader was killed." To her surprise, the young man began to cry as he said, "Ma'am, you're the first person who has let me come into their house this morning. I was afraid I was going to lose my job."

That first night was only the beginning of the flood of racial violence and hatred. Along with a lot of other manifestations of hatred and bitterness, stones were thrown at the church, firebombs were planted, and bricks were tossed through the windows. The worst incident came the day my sister-in-law, Clariece, who was serving as treasurer for the church, was working in the church office with me. We heard a gunshot, and then we looked up at the church office window. A bullet had pierced the window glass just over the top of Clariece's head and passed right over my head to lodge itself in the wall right behind me. Someone also tried to set the church on fire during that period.

At home our telephone rang constantly for several weeks, and Norma had to tell our girls not to answer the telephone anymore. Much of the time, the language was so vulgar and hateful that I could not bear for my daughters to hear it. We had enemies of both sides of the "color line," and we were called "nigger lovers" and every vile name in the book.

All of this was just a part of the explosive spirit that permeated the city of Atlanta at that time. Many innocent people were hurt. Some of us who were very much involved in the battle to bring about racial harmony were attacked and accused of being racists. People just didn't know what they were doing and saying.

For better or for worse, the untimely death of Martin Luther King, Jr., brought about a new day in the Civil Rights Movement. Some of the young leaders who had become our friends carried on Dr. King's vision of a nonviolent revolution of the heart, but there was much striving over who would lead the floundering movement. Through it all, it was obvious to everyone that the charisma, the anointing, the passion, and the vision that were resident in Martin Luther King, Jr., was gone.

Some of the men who maintained the spirit and vision that Dr. King had begun remain our friends to this day. Foremost among these friends is Andrew Young, the brilliant preacher who went on to become Ambassador to the United Nations under President Jimmy Carter, and who later became Mayor of Atlanta. He still speaks to our congregation as his schedule permits. Two of these occasions particularly blessed me. First, he honored me by attending a banquet recognizing my fiftieth year in the ministry; and second, he visited our church to share his excitement with our people when it was announced that Atlanta had been selected as the site of the 1996 Olympic games.

Through the years, our choirs, dancers, and orchestra have all participated in the many "Kingfest" art programs, and we were especially honored by an invitation to be featured as "the church that was deemed the expression of Martin Luther King, Jr.'s dream" on a parade float on his birthday. The whole world saw our integrated choir worshiping God with joy on television that day.

As surely as God lives, I will continue to remain faithful to my vow to Sammy in the cotton fields of South Georgia: "Sammy, I'll make it up to you."

Free At Last

(Reba Rambo/Dony McGuire, New Kingdom Music/ASCAP ©1984. Used with permission.)

CHORUS:
Free at last, it is finished
Life has triumphed over death
Jesus reigns, bless the name of God Almighty
Free at last

Shout out our independence
Slaves that now are kings
Worship our liberator
Let's lift our voice and sing

Free at last, it is finished
Life has triumphed over death
Jesus reigns, bless the name of God Almighty
Free at last

Chapter 3

We Have to Stay the Course

By the year 1971, we had been in the Little Five Points area of Atlanta for 11 years. Now we had to decide whether we should move or not. The state highway department had built a highway right through the middle of the community we served. For the most part the population was moving out, even though we were still enjoying some growth. Almost all of the churches in the neighborhood had already left, and some of the members of those churches had come to worship with us. Still, it seemed absolutely necessary for us to make a move.

This was extremely difficult for me to accept because I felt God had put us in this particular place in the 1960's. At the same time, I knew something new was about to happen. I had to have a "sure word" from God. Some of the church members were recommending a six-acre tract of land in South DeKalb County, which was about 20 minutes away by car. I went out to see the land, and as I walked onto the six-acre tract, I was feeling the pressure to make a definite decision about the move.

I climbed a small hill and knelt down beside a little pine tree to pray. As I broke off a small twig, the Spirit of the Lord spoke distinctly to my spirit. Yes, somehow I knew this was the place where God was leading us. Years later, I heard prophets who knew nothing about our promise from God echo these ancient words of Ezekiel the prophet, the same words that God brought to me that day by the pine tree:

Thus says the Lord God: "I Myself will take a sprig from the lofty top of the cedar, and will set it out; I will break off from the topmost of its young twigs a tender one, and I Myself will plant it upon a high and lofty mountain; on the mountain height of Israel will I plant it, that it may bring forth boughs and bear fruit, and become a noble cedar; and under it will dwell all kinds of beasts; in the shade of its branches birds of every sort will nest. And all the trees of the field shall know that I the Lord bring low the high tree, and make high the low tree, dry up the green tree, and make the dry tree flourish. I the Lord have spoken, and I will do it" (Ezekiel 17:22-24 RSV).

I announced the decision and we began to build a very modest sanctuary on the site. Despite our great reluctance to leave the site of our small beginning, the day came when we made our move from Little Five Points out to South DeKalb in January, 1972. Our new neighborhood was "almost totally white," and the people living there tended to be very conservative. Many of them were Baptists, a number were Methodists, and there were even a few Presbyterians and some members of the Christian Church sprinkled throughout the area for good measure.

After our first attempt at "integration" with the imported African university students, we desperately tried to maintain some measure of integration, but without success. When we moved to South DeKalb, we desperately prayed that the Lord would give us an opportunity to face the racial issue with visible action, not mere words. We had quickly learned that having a truly integrated church is more than just having blacks and whites (or any two nationalities for that matter) meeting together in the same building. Integration demanded that we build relationships and live together in the same community. It demanded that we really get to know each other. Clariece Paulk, my sister-in-law, is known for her saying, "People don't know what they like—they like what they know."

Shortly after we relocated, we began to see a few black believers slip into our congregation. (I am sure we were overly friendly with them.) It wasn't long before a black sister started singing in the choir; and then a black brother joined the ushers. Little by little, our congregation began to be truly integrated. We began to be very conscious of our new members' presence, and we began to worship and sing in a way we felt would be pleasing to God, yet be meaningful to all the members of our congregation.

As our church began to grow very rapidly, we began to have two worship services on Sunday morning and another service on Sunday evening to accommodate the needs of the people.

The Holy Spirit began moving through the young people in the church, and they began a ministry called "Alpha," named after the new life we receive in Jesus Christ. They formed a Christian musical rock group of the same name and hundreds of teenagers from high schools all over the city attended a Monday evening youth service at the church.

Another source of growth was the powerful ministry of spiritual deliverance God brought to us through the dedicated ministry of a young woman who had moved down from Baltimore, Maryland. Lynn Mays clearly had a real gift of spiritual discernment and deliverance, and at our invitation, she soon joined our staff. Her ministry to people searching for answers to their needs brought many new members to our church.

The life-changing ministry to teenagers and to hurting people needing deliverance and healing caused our fellowship to quickly swell to over 1,000 members. However, a third factor would soon trigger an incredibly explosive growth rate for our church family.

The growth I am talking about was "rapid growth." First we rejoiced over reaching the 1,000-member mark, knowing that God had sovereignly done it all. Then we quickly grew to 2,000 members, and before long we had 5,000 members. It was about that time that we began to notice that many of the white people living nearby were moving out of our area. Frankly, we began to see a real "white flight." As fast as the white people moved out, we saw black people moving in. The black community in our church grew rapidly until approximately 40 percent of our congregation was black. We realized we had to enlarge our facilities.

An all-white Baptist church was located across the street from us. One day the pastor of that church came over to see me. He told me they were interested in selling their property. He asked if we might be interested in purchasing it, or if we might know someone who would be interested. Now that the community had changed, they wanted to move out of the community. I felt it was a good deal, so we started making arrangements to purchase the property.

We launched a private Christian school, Cathedral Academy, and based it in the former Baptist church building and the adjoining Sunday school building and gymnasium. It was founded from the beginning as an integrated school, and we have always encouraged students from all races to attend. It has become a great institution in our community. Dozens of students whose families could not afford to send their children to a Christian school were given scholarships. To date, all of our graduates have gone on to college, with the exception of two who went into the armed forces. Many have received full or partial scholarships to major universities in America.

One of our black students, Lewis Lamar, Jr., has now graduated from the University of New Mexico where he won acclaim playing NCAA Division I basketball. His athletic training began at Cathedral Academy where he played high school basketball with Donnie Earl Paulk, the son of Don and Clariece. Because he lived a great distance from the school and did not have transportation at the time, he lived with the Paulks all during high school, and is like a brother to Donnie Earl to this day.

Adjoining our property on Flat Shoals Road was an Assembly of God church. Again, the pastor of this congregation came to see me one day and said they were going to be moving out. He also asked me if we wanted to purchase their property. At that time we did not need more property, but we felt it was important to purchase the Assembly of God property for the future. We managed to purchase the property with great sacrifice, and it became our Bible Institute.

Pressures continued to grow as the neighborhood underwent rapid and radical transformation. Still we stayed in the community. It was my personal conviction that God had planted us there, and the only right thing to do was to stay where He had placed us. Not only did we stay in the community, but we made it known in every way possible that we were staying because we believed God wanted a church in the community that could stand and be a "church of one blood." After all, this was what the Word of God teaches.

Then I received a visit from Dr. Kirby Clements, a very outstanding black dentist. He let me know that his vision coincided with ours, and soon he became a member of our staff. He served as a local pastor on our staff for many years, and he now represents the Office of the Bishop to our networking churches across the country and the world. Dr. Clements played a very vital role because he was a highly visible leader from the black community.

People throughout Atlanta began to see that our "integrated" church also had truly integrated leadership. We added a number of deacons to our leadership who happened to be from the black community; and our choir became very strongly integrated with many soloists from the black culture. Our leadership role in areas of racial conflict and reconciliation reached new levels of visibility.

Then came the nightmare of 1979, marking one of the saddest years on record for Atlanta, Georgia. The national television networks and newspapers around the world began to run front-page headlines about the serial killer who was killing black children in Atlanta.

Black children in Atlanta, primarily boys, began to mysteriously disappear while on their way home from school, or while playing outside their own homes. The bodies of many of these innocent victims were found days later, floating down a river or thrown into a wooded area, over a two-year period. Black parents became very fearful for their children's safety, and the entire city lived under a strict curfew regulating children in public places.

Then I received a call from my friend, Dr. Frazier Ben Todd, the head of the Atlanta branch of the NAACP (National Association for the Advancement of Colored People). He asked me if I was willing to get involved. (I think he already knew my answer.) On February 14, 1981, I made a television appeal to the killer or killers of the Atlanta children at the end of our weekly television program. That day, the church ran and paid for a full-page advertisement in the *Atlanta Journal* and the *Atlanta Constitution* that said, "If you are responsible for the crimes against our children, this television appeal is to you. Watch Saturday, February 14, Channel 46 at 11:00 p.m."

I pleaded with the killer during that program. "End this nightmare and come forward. Ease your tormented mind. I promise that I will mediate communication between you and the police. I assure you that you can speak to me in all privacy, and that Jesus Christ loves you and is willing to forgive you for what you've done. We will even give you a public platform to give your grievances to this city—we want to help you."

The very next day, phone calls began coming from supposed killers. Many of these were prank calls, but on February 16th, we received a series of calls that never lasted more than a few seconds. When the mysterious caller instructed me to go to a local television station for the 6 o'clock evening news broadcast, Don and I went down to the station. Later on, the same person called back and said, "Well, I didn't see you on camera."

What he wanted me to do was be there on camera so he could either show up personally or telephone me while I was on camera so we could conduct an on-the-air telephone conversation. A lot of that was unclear, but the police knew all about the phone calls and the caller's requests. We made sure they knew everything we were doing.

The following Sunday afternoon, I preached at a citywide prayer meeting held at the request of the NAACP. I preached from the passage in chapter 6 of the Book of Ephesians, emphasizing the battle between God and the powers and principalities of the air, between darkness and light. On Monday, someone interrupted our staff meeting to say someone was on the phone who was identifying himself as "the one Earl Paulk is trying to reach." I rushed to the phone, but only a few seconds after I identified myself, he hung up. An hour later he called back again, but he refused to set a time and place for a meeting.

Finally the caller described a particular van and told us to look for it on a certain night in the vicinity of the church, so Don and I parked near our chapel and waited. We saw a van drive up into the parking lot of our school, which is situated across the street from the church. The van matched the vehicle described by the mysterious caller. We started across the street to meet the person or persons as we had promised. At that moment, another car suddenly pulled into the lot. I don't know to this day whether it was the Secret Service, the FBI, or what. Then two more cars pulled into the lot where the van was. Just as suddenly as the van appeared, the driver spun his tires and disappeared, moving so quickly we couldn't even see the license tag. I never knew if it was the killer who was involved in the incident that night, but the other men involved were plainclothes officers of some kind.

Then one night, the mysterious caller phoned again and asked us to come to a truck stop at the edge of town. Don and I went alone with no weapons. I still think the call was legitimate, but we'll never know. When I got out there with Don and pulled up to this place, there were cars everywhere! The law enforcement officials had obviously been listening in on our conversation with the caller, and I had no problem with that. However, if the caller would have come, he would have been a fool—he would have certainly been shot in that crowded parking lot. Unfortunately, we will never know whether or not it was the killer who called.

The FBI stepped in at the request of the media, and Federal agents stayed around the church property for several weeks conducting round-the-clock surveillance. An FBI agent talked to me about what they were going to do, and we didn't have a choice in it. I was simply told, "We will be covering all your phone lines and monitoring all of your conversations."

Three months before the twentieth victim was murdered, someone called in with a threat: "The next victim will be white." The caller may have been a prankster, but whoever had called wanted the white staff members at Harvester Church to believe it was going to be "one of us." Many of the parents in our church family still remember the tension they felt as they took every precaution to protect their children during those years and months of terror.

On February 28th, I made another appeal on the "Harvester Hour" television broadcast, and as a result, the same mysterious caller talked to me for the last time. Three days later, the twentieth victim was found. The killer had dumped the body of the child just over the hill within view of the church. The child's body was found on March 6th, caught on a log in the South River, just a quarter of a mile from our church sanctuary. Our church family took it as a direct affront toward us.

The national network news coverage intensified, and I called for a 24-hour prayer vigil in concert with other churches in the area to intercede for a swift end to the crimes. The warfare was clearly kingdom against kingdom.

Within a few months, a suspect was arrested and later convicted for committing two of the crimes, with "incomplete but related evidence" in the other cases. No one knows if the suspect was the murderer or not, but we do know that the murders ceased after the man's arrest. Ironically, the suspect the police apprehended was a black man. To this day the man still claims that he is innocent, and though I doubt his claim, I have always believed that there were more people involved.

The members of our congregation were deeply grieved over the murders. It is impossible to express how hurt and empathetic the people were over the loss of those innocent children. Yet they never hesitated or wavered in their support of our involvement in the crisis.

People outside the church responded to what we had done in different ways. Most people were very grateful, and an overwhelming majority of the letters and calls we received were favorable. The NAACP deeply appreciated our efforts to help calm both the black and white residents of Atlanta during the crisis, but a few callers were convinced that we were trying to become "overnight celebrities" by capitalizing on the plight of the murdered children.

This perspective was tragic, but even more importantly, it revealed some serious attitudes and prejudices that went far beyond the issue of the serial killer. Many people resent a pastor, or church congregation, who takes social action during challenging life-and-death situations. In their minds, society demands a church that "assumes a passive, peaceful, Santa Claus-like role" toward social problems.

Many Christians are asking themselves today, "How can we integrate our church?" Others just want to have some "token representatives" of other races in their church body to soothe their consciences. A few want to integrate their churches so they can experience sudden growth, but I tell them, "Unless it is a part of your conviction, it not only will not work, but it also will not last." Without apology, I say, "I do not believe in black churches or white churches—I believe in Christian churches." If 75 percent of the Christians in a city, region, or nation are black, then the same percentage of people in the church should probably be black. If only ten percent of the people within a hundred-mile radius of a church are Hispanic, then about ten percent of that church's congregation should be Hispanic.

However, I have a problem with single-race churches serving communities where people of all nationalities live within driving distance. There is no excuse for a church not to be integrated! It is my heartfelt conviction that the very essence of Pentecost was demonstrated when people from every nation gathered together in Jerusalem and were moved upon by the Spirit of God. That marked God's sovereign and eternal reversal of the travesty of racial division birthed at Babel.[1]

---

1. Acts 2:5-11.

We underwent great persecution at times from within and without over our commitment to a "church of one blood," but our congregation not only maintained its vitality, it also managed to grow despite the opposition of countless circumstances over the years. Today we number over 12,000 people of nearly every conceivable race and culture!

No other white or integrated congregation remains in our community today. Many of the so-called white churches sold their buildings to black congregations, or in some cases, denominational leaders simply appointed black pastors to pastor all-black congregations. This always grieved my heart. I always felt there was no reason in the world for people to move away. The truth is that they simply did not want to live with black people in peace.

To maintain integration in our community, we bought acreage and sold it to builders in our church. They built houses and condos and we controlled their racial balance. We offered different price ranges to make them available for everyone.

We felt God had planted us in this community for a purpose, and as we walked out that purpose, we realized we had to build more facilities. First we built the "K-Center" (or "Kingdom Center"), but we quickly outgrew it. Then we added the Atrium to the complex, but again everything was full and overflowing. Then God spoke to us to build the Cathedral.

A cathedral is traditionally understood to be a "seat of authority" or a place that is the home or base for the spiritual office of a bishop. I had been consecrated to the office of bishop at the hands of Bishop Robert McAlister from Brazil years before. I wouldn't even let the people in the church or ministry staff call me "bishop" for the first year after I had been installed. But then we started adding churches to our association family from all over, and I realized it was a legitimate title. We were now "pastoring pastors," and the office of bishop was the office of an overseer. I finally got comfortable with the title after I had been doing the "job" for some years. (Now as a member of the College of Bishops of the International Communion of Charismatic Churches, we oversee several million members and hundreds of pastors.)

Many people felt it was totally wrong to build a "cathedral" in a community where there didn't seem to be a need or even an appreciation for it.

It is odd that a cathedral was not considered unusual in Buckhead or some other affluent Atlanta community, but it was certainly not acceptable in South DeKalb.

"Acceptable" or not, the cathedral began to rise, and we saw that God was in it. We felt we should call it The Cathedral of the Holy Spirit, and it has become a landmark in this area, as well as one of the best-known institutions in the South and in the nation, along with our school. The Cathedral is often filled with people from many nations who have come to worship and praise God as a people of one blood. It isn't unusual to have nationally respected speakers such as Bishop T.D. Jakes, or Marvin Winans, or Carlton Pearson one week, and the next week to have E.V. Hill, Mark Hanby, Terry Crist, Tommy Reid, or perhaps Bishop Perez from Venezuela, or Archbishop Benson Idahosa from Nigeria. We have even had the great bishop of the Methodist Church, Dr. William Cannon.

What a joy it is to share the Cathedral with others—Spellman College (Commencement), Georgia G.E.D. (Commencement), famous lecturer and environmentalist, Jon Cousteau—or to fill the Cathedral with great music during the live recordings of Richard Smallwood and James Bignon.

It is a thrill to see the Cathedral filled with people from so many nations of the earth, because I am convinced that this is truly "Pentecostal" in the biblical sense. I believe that the miracle of the "Azusa Outpouring" is still remembered today more than the move among classical Pentecostal churches because it began as a move of God upon an integrated group of people.

I hear a lot of preachers discuss the racial problem today, and at times it grieves my heart. I'm not troubled because they are concerned—that is good. I'm concerned because it is obvious they do not understand the problem. Racial integration or reconciliation does not have to do with people of different colors sitting in the same building—it is a blending of hearts.

Most of these discussions are shallow at best. Like so many of our politicians, most of these ministers think that you can prescribe a policy and pass legislation that will integrate a society, and that's impossible. You may be able to make people stay in the same geographical area, but you can't integrate them. First of all, integration must begin as a deep conviction of the heart. Secondly, it must be lived out in terms of real human relationships. I remember the day Martin Luther King, Jr., said, "The race situation as we know it will never be resolved at the food counter, the schools, or the business place." Then he looked in my direction and said, "It will only be resolved when it passes through the kitchen and gets into the bedroom."

Dr. King was saying that genuine integration and reconciliation will only come out of relationships. Ironically, it is the concept of "relationships" that scares white people the most. They are afraid their kid will marry a black person. That basic fear even caused some problems in our church about five years ago. When the church leadership dealt with a moral problem according to biblical standards, a number of our white members used that as a pretext to leave the church. Yet we knew most of those people hadn't left because of a moral problem confessed by a man in our ministry—that was dealt with openly, biblically, and compassionately.

The truth was that those who left were not able to handle the integration that was taking place, particularly among their teenage children. There was beginning to be some interracial dating, and these white parents were looking for any excuse to leave without revealing their real concern. Hundreds of people left under the guise that they were disappointed with the leadership.

The truth is that the moral issue was never the problem. If that were the issue, then the Word of God is not at all properly understood. God's Word declares that when a sin is confessed, whether it is in the pulpit or pew, it must be forgiven. The real problem had to do with the fact that many of our white people simply could not handle the racial problem.

I thank God for the thousands of people who endured the storm and who remain a vital part of our ministry today. The exciting part of this ongoing story is that our black community not only has grown, but also plays a vital part in what is going on today in every area of our church life. Hundreds have been added to our fellowship recently, including many whites.

Some things simply cannot be legislated. It always struck me as being odd that the U.S. Government thought hauling kids in buses from one part of town to another would "integrate" public schools. The hope of integration was good, but the method will never work because it doesn't cause integration to take place from the heart or from actual conviction. This is not a matter for government to try to control. It is a matter that can only be dealt with through the conscience of men. That is why the Church ought to speak prophetically into these situations.

Human governments will never be able to control race problems because these problems are spiritual in nature. Racial strife and hatred aren't merely problems that have to do with division by location.

I have great admiration for both Billy Graham and Oral Roberts. Both of these evangelists not only preached about the rights of all people to attend their meetings early on in the history of their crusades, but they also practiced it. This was a step in the right direction and should be remembered as a step forward in handling the racial problem. Even unto this present hour, Billy Graham's citywide crusades are conducted for all people, and Oral Roberts University in Tulsa, Oklahoma, has a truly multiracial and multinational student body composed of people from nations around the world.

All too often, we feel we can "handle" things like the racial problem because we are not personally involved in them. However, once the problem "comes home to roost" in our own home or among our own children, it becomes a different matter!

I truly believe that as this planet grows smaller and smaller, particularly in a nation as amalgamated as the United States, it will become absolutely necessary for us to face the racial issue head on, and realize the solutions are only found in God.

I was recently invited to return to my alma mater, Emory University, to speak to the students at the Candler School of Theology. The class, which appeared to contain equal numbers of white and black students, was under the instruction of a respected professor named Dr. Noel Erskine (who happens to be black). I had been asked to speak about the "theology" of Martin Luther King, Jr.

Martin Luther King, Jr., never wrote a theological book *per se*, but what he believed was woven throughout his writings, including his concepts of God, of nature, and of man. He was a man who had been uniquely created "for such a time as this." He began his studies at Atlanta's Morehouse College, then earned a Master's degree at Grozier Seminary. He rounded out his education by earning a doctorate at Boston University.

His extensive study at universities in the North gave him a broad perspective of God's work in the world. That broad view of history can be seen creeping into his preaching and teaching across the years. His excellent education, combined with his strong family ties with Daddy King, who was a great preacher, made him the great leader who was able to change the course of a nation through the force of his personal God-given conviction.

At the end of my discourse, someone asked the question, "What would Martin Luther Jr. have said about the Million Man March sponsored by Mr. Farrakhan?" I quickly replied out of my conviction:

"If Martin Luther King, Jr., were still alive, there would not have been a Million Man March under Louis Farrakhan in Washington! Martin Luther King, Jr., did not believe in what is called 'black power' or militancy. He not only believed in a nonviolent approach to the problems, but he also felt the solution was based in God.

"Properly understood, the Civil Rights Movement was not a movement that had to do at all with government involvement; it had to do with a spiritual revival that took place in the hearts of spiritual leaders. Martin Luther King, Jr., was a mighty preacher of the Word, and this was his platform and his background, and the power of his life and ministry.

"May I add that some of the great leaders such as Ralph Abernathy and certainly Andrew Young were first and foremost, great preachers. Every time Andrew Young fills our pulpit, our people thrill to hear the gospel. It is well to note that many of the Civil Rights leaders of that day were really great men and women of God who had a great anointing. When the movement became something that was handled more from a governmental standpoint, it began to die in its prominence. At that time there was a vacuum or void left for other leaders to move in who oftentimes did not understand what God was doing at all."

I am thankful for the groundwork laid by the sacrifice and courage of men like Martin Luther King, Jr., who dared to invest their lives in a heavenly dream. I rejoice in the belief that something seems to be taking place in the hearts of many leaders in America. I believe that with the guidance of the Holy Spirit and with the Church maintaining its prophetic posture, positive movement can take place. But there must not only be a new love one for another—we must also search the Word of God for the real truth about prejudice. We must realize that God has, in fact, made us "one blood as a Church, and as one spiritual nation."

The March Goes On
(Anthony Lockett, Cathedral Praise Publ. ©1990. Used with permission.)

We've marched in the streets
Bearing love on our feet
As one holy troop spreading the gospel of truth.

We've committed our lives to unify
Every heart and mind in the name of Christ.

CHORUS:
The march goes on,
The march goes on,
From glory to glory
From victory to victory
The march goes on.

The color of heart is all that we see.
And we stand to agree that all men shall be free.
We stand to fight,
We shine forth our light.
It's not by our might
But by the Spirit of Christ.

There's a new dimension,
Of battle at hand—
A battle of spirits
Within the hearts of men.
We're prepared for war,
In full armor we stand,
Ready to march
At the Master's command.

Chapter 4

The Problem With People (and the Cure)

"Reverse prejudice" is a very negative term to the African-American community, yet according to James Powers, one of the black pastors at the Cathedral, this term may be appropriately applied to what is taking place in our community today.

At one time certain people were asking us for help, and today those same people—who are now leaders in the black community—have very little patience with their white brethren. Many of the black believers who attend our church are ridiculed and attacked by other blacks in the community for attending a church "pastored by a white pastor." Many of these critics do not know how many times I publicly put my life and ministry in jeopardy to uphold the convictions I have about racial justice.

I've found that the "love of money" is often at the root of these problems. When a congregation loses members, it affects the budget. There is a strong temptation to regard any person, organization, or thing that "attracts people and their money," with a great deal of animosity.

However, there are some things that we should look at very carefully and with an open mind. When a contest is held for a Black Miss America, this maintains the institution of segregation, but from a different point of view. The much-publicized "Million Man March" in Washington was billed as a million "black men" marching instead of a million men who had a conviction against racial prejudice.

I understand that the format included messages about what black men could do for themselves, but overall, this march was a political move to the heart and core. Its agenda was separation and elevation, not integration and equality.

A black minister named Carlton Pearson recently told our congregation in the Cathedral that Jesse Jackson could come into a church and register people to vote in the same way that old-fashioned evangelists used to lead people to Jesus. For example, he would say, "All of you here who are not registered to vote, please hold up your hand!" Then he would say, "Will you please stand?" Finally he would conclude by saying, "Will you please come forward? We want to register you to vote."

The hard reality is that while this kind of thing is openly condoned in black churches, it could not take place in a white church. The doors of the church would be quickly closed and locked by state and Federal watchdogs determined to shut down any "political action" in a church to preserve their notion of the "separation of church and state."

Every area and activity that continues to foster the separation and inequitable treatment of the races must be addressed honestly. We create another set of problems through our tendency to cling to false ideas and stereotypes about likes and dislikes of people of different races or cultures in worship services. For the last two Christmases, the Atlanta Symphony has presented concerts in the Cathedral. Our congregation is now composed of more blacks than whites, yet they thoroughly enjoy this music. Some view classical music as being something only enjoyed by white people, but this is simply not true.

We tend to prefer what we have been raised with and what we know best. It is an "acceptable" practice for a basically white congregation to invite black artists to sing and minister in their meetings. However, when that congregation goes a step further and begins to be integrated, many people want to draw the line when kids of different races begin to have an interest in one another. This is considered totally unacceptable. My question is, "Why? Show the problem to me in God's Word." Until this is viewed from a Christian perspective with the Bible as our guide, there will never be a real solution to the race problem. We need to recognize the difference between biblical standards and social whims.

I often hear the complaint, "You are trying to integrate families and encourage interracial marriages!" This is not true—I am only trying to follow what the Bible says. God has not said or even suggested anywhere in His Word that there should not be interracial marriages—He simply says we should not be joined to unbelievers.[1] Unfortunately, some people want their child to marry a person of their own race—even if that person is an unbeliever! This is not only in direct conflict with the Word of God, but in eternity, is very destructive for the salvation of the soul. I think this attitude indicates we've lost our grip on reality and the really important values in life.

I have to emphasize again that from my personal knowledge of Martin Luther King, Jr., he was not interested in promoting what some call "black power." He was out to resolve the differences between the races in a Christian fashion. Over and over again, he talked about having a dream. If you examine his dream very carefully, you will see that he dreamed that "little black boys and girls, and little white boys and girls, would join hands and walk together across the muddy hills of Georgia and attend the same schools." This was the heart cry of Martin Luther King, Jr. If he were alive today, I believe he would still be pointing out the inconsistencies of our actions toward other races. They are still very prevalent, though they may be more subtle.

I make it abundantly clear at the Cathedral and in the ministry that we do not choose candidates for positions on the staff or the presbytery "because they are black" or "because they are white." We choose people solely "because they are qualified" for the assignment or job. Unfortunately, some people in our nation use the term "qualified" to slyly suggest that some "special effort" is needed to find qualified blacks, while qualified whites are relatively easy to find. This may be an indirect racial slur, but it clearly points to an underlying ideology or theory that is both ungodly and racist.

I'm going into all this because our beliefs are manifested by our works. The way we speak and act toward one another presents a generally accurate picture of the way we think and believe on the inside. My definition of "qualification" at the Cathedral consists of two conditions: a) a personal commitment to Christ, and b) the ability to do the job. Qualification consists of nothing more and nothing less.

Yes, I am sensitive to the way our staff and presbytery should look based on our call to demonstrate a Spirit-filled integrated environment

---

1.   Deuteronomy 7:3-4; 2 Corinthians 6:14-17.

before the world. Yet, I also know that the very moment we try to "balance things" based on race or any other outward criteria, we have made a grave error.

We must allow the Word of God to wash away the humanist idea that God sees color as a factor in making distinctions in the human family. He sees color only as a factor in the beauty of His creation. God does not choose to see us as white humans, black humans, Hispanic humans, or humans of some specific national origin. He sees us as individual sons and daughters of Adam and Eve who stand in need of salvation and restoration through the blood of His Son.

As long as we view people as human beings instead of members of a particular race, we are on our way to making genuine progress. God sees us as potential sons and daughters of the Kingdom, His chosen people. Peter said, "...in time past [we] were not a people, but are now the people of God."[2] How should God's chosen people look? They will look like a rainbow, for they will be drawn from every nation and every tongue under the sun. Eventually they will live together in the very presence of God.

The other day someone was talking to me about a great preacher, and the person asked me if I had met him. I answered, "Yes, I have met him. And he is, in fact, a great minister of the gospel." Immediately, the person's next question was, "Is he black or white?" At that point, I have to confess, a very stubborn streak hit me and my reply was, "I didn't really notice."

We encounter the same kind of prejudices against women. It's common to have a great woman preacher come among us and afterward hear someone say, "That was the greatest woman preacher I have ever heard." Now think about this: How many times have you ever heard someone say of a woman preacher, "That was the greatest preacher I have ever heard"?

Several years ago, we invited Iverna Tompkins to minister in our church. Afterward, I heard many of the people talking about her, and referring to her as the greatest woman preacher they had ever heard. Then I said from my pulpit one day (without any apology), "Iverna Tompkins is one of the greatest preachers—period—that I have ever heard preach the gospel of the Lord Jesus Christ."

---

2.   1 Peter 2:10a.

When a "qualified" reference is made to a black preacher, a woman preacher, a black doctor, or a woman doctor, those innocuous little "qualifier" words specifying race or gender take away from the person's true professional status or calling. Most people (including some women and minorities) believe that somehow, for some reason, preachers and doctors who are black are not comparable to those who are white. It is too easy to see things through prejudice-tainted glasses, rather than to see each human being for what he or she is really worth! This is true for the Kingdom of God as well as for human institutions and roles.

I felt prompted by the Spirit of God to publicly demonstrate my love for people of all races during a worship service attended by several thousand people. It wasn't done for show or for public relations; it was an act of obedience. I abruptly stopped my sermon in the middle of the service and invited a young black man to come to the pulpit and sit in a seat. Then I sent for a water basin, dropped to my knees, gently pulled off his shoes, and washed and dried his feet.

I did this not only as a symbol of my love for this man and for the black race, but also to show that this was the true spirit of what the Christian life is all about. As long as we are washing "black feet" or "white feet," we are making a mistake. Once we understand that we are simply washing feet, and that we are wiping away the soil and the pollution that comes from the world, then we are demonstrating that we are a peculiar people according to the Word of the Lord. There is nothing more peculiar about us than the fact that we hold absolutely no prejudices against one another.

Jesus recognized and ruthlessly confronted the spirit of prejudice that had historically divided the Jews from the Samaritans. He gave us two very glaring examples of how to deal with this problem. First, He described the Jew who was traveling from Jerusalem to Jericho and fell among thieves.[3] He pointedly described the way two Jewish religious leaders carefully walked "on the other side" of the road from the fallen man to avoid contamination.

The helpless victim was a member of their own race, but he had fallen in the ditch and was bloody and dirty. Then a man Jesus called a "certain Samaritan" came down the road. He not only went into the ditch and recovered

3.   Luke 10:30-37.

the man, but he also put the victim on his own mount and led him to a road-side inn where his wounds could be tended and healed. He even told the innkeeper, "Take care of him and I will pay the bill." Jesus praised this good Samaritan because he had a heart to reach out to anyone, regardless of his national origin.

Even more outrageous was Jesus' encounter with the woman of Samaria at the well.[4] He broke the time-honored prejudiced customs of His day just by speaking to a woman in a public place. Even worse, He dared to speak to a Samaritan woman who had an immoral reputation! His disciples could not understand why their great Teacher was socializing with such a sinful woman from a second-rate race.

Here again, Jesus went out of His way to break down barriers and prejudices against people who were in sin. Think about this: Jesus clearly knew that the Samaritan woman had been married five times, and was living with a man to whom she was not married. How did He handle this problem? How would we handle it today?

Did He condemn her for her obvious sin? No. Did He command her to go and straighten out the matter of her former husbands? No; He didn't even tell her to leave the man with whom she was living. He simply gave her "Living Water" to satisfy her thirst. How could He overlook this woman's obvious sins and shortcomings? He knew that once this woman's thirst was satisfied, she would automatically straighten out her relationships.

The same thing is true about our racial problems today! Once we really submit to and walk in the will and mind of God, then we will suddenly recognize that prejudice is not the problem. We simply lack a pure conscience and a pure heart before God.

Jesus went out of His way to break down every barrier placed between people over economic, racial, religious, or social differences and prejudices. He specifically called Matthew as His disciple, even though the man was a hated tax collector and Roman collaborator.[5] He also went to the home of Zaccheus, a man who was deeply and bitterly hated by his fellow Jews because of his occupation and unethical business practices.[6]

---

4.   John 4:4-42.
5.   Matthew 9:9.
6.   Luke 19:2-10.

Many of us are prejudiced against certain people for reasons we can't even explain! The true Christian spirit not only jumps the obstacles that separate the human race into groups, but also reaches out to others with tremendous compassion.

During the time when much was being said across the nation about abortion, we launched a ministry we called the "House of New Life." We provided housing, food, clothing, love, and teaching for unwed pregnant girls, and we stayed with them until they had delivered their babies. We also set up a Christian adoption agency so we could arrange for many of these children to be adopted into loving Christian families.

At the same time, we were also criticized because we would not participate in some of the demonstrations against medical facilities performing abortions. Frankly, this seemed foolish to us because all that these demonstrations seemed to do was cause more problems for the young women who were already being destroyed.

It seemed to me to be far more valuable to conduct such demonstrations where the appropriate medical authorities were. It is important to express your displeasure about the abortions to those with the power to change the situation, rather than afflict those who are already victims. While I understand the desire to save the innocent children in the wombs of those women, I still think that a better way to effect long-term change is to speak to the people involved in the governmental aspects of this action.

Too often we preach to people who have no power to change or correct a problem. For example, why should we preach against the problems in public education in our churches, when we could begin to correct the problem by talking to the school board or the school superintendent? If I have a problem with the city government, I make no apology for speaking to the mayor or the city council face to face.

When we discovered that teenagers were being served drinks in certain establishments near the Cathedral, I immediately called the Commissioner of Public Safety. We discussed the problem, and I asked him what we could do about this. At the time of this writing, it can now be disclosed that certain members of our youth group volunteered to work undercover with law enforcement officials and help catch the offenders in the act and bring them to justice. We no longer have that particular problem in our area because we directed our protest to the right person and agency.

Over and over again, Jesus spoke to people who really had power over given problems. He publicly confronted the scribes and Pharisees, and even called them "vipers" and "whited sepulchers."[7] When He saw a sinner who had fallen by the wayside, He reached out with great compassion and love—even when the sinner was a harlot.[8]

The only way to deal correctly with the problems at hand is to determine where the actual power lies, and then begin to deal with the issue in the proper fashion and order by talking to the proper person or agency involved.

I am saddened when I hear preachers eloquently present ways to handle racial problems when all the while I know in my heart that, back in their own pastorate, they do not practice what they preach!

The hour has arrived for us to take a stand without apology. I have worked with many organizations over the years to help promote the work of the Kingdom of God. I was one of the founders of the Network of Christian Ministries (NCM) several years ago. When Dr. Oral Roberts founded the International Charismatic Bible Ministries (ICBM), I was one of the original trustees. For a number of years, I have been a part of Churches United in Global Mission, which is a ministry begun by Dr. Robert Schuller.

All of these are great organizations and moves of God. I most recently made myself available to the "Azusa Conference." I made it clear to the leaders of the Azusa movement that I wanted to help keep their movement from becoming primarily a "black movement." This great move of the Spirit can only be properly understood as a multinational outpouring of God upon all flesh.

We need to hear far less preaching about our roots and more talk about our fruit. It is far more important to understand where we are going than to focus on where we came from and where we are presently. No one, not even God Himself, can change the past. Of course it is important to know where we came from and to have a personal identity—I have no problem with this concept at all. Although it is important for each of us to know the value of his family tree or natural origin, we cannot let this natural "bloodline" sidetrack us from the truth and supreme value of our inheritance in the spiritual family of God and the blood of Christ.

7.   Matthew 23:13-36.
8.   John 8:3-11.

In the past, many white Americans shared with their children a "family tree" that often would extend far beyond the borders and history of the United States. Black parents, however, could only give their children a heritage and family tree rooted in the negativity and sorrow of slavery. They often had to locate their ancestors among the same records slave owners used to keep track of their farm animals.

When the early stereotype of black Americans being descendants of the "backward, uncivilized, and dark continent of Africa" gave way to the accurate understanding of that continent's diverse tribal histories and ancient heritage, blacks began to appreciate their homeland and its historical contributions to the world. It became both popular and expedient for many blacks to trace their family roots. Some went to extremes and began using this information to establish the idea of black "racial superiority." This is just as wrong as the efforts of white groups to try to establish white racial superiority.

I don't believe that we need to teach "black history" one month or one week in the year. We need to teach true "human history" 52 weeks a year! I am not against people knowing their natural roots, but once we have been purged with the blood of Jesus Christ, we must lay aside our strife and embrace our Christian brothers and sisters, regardless of their race.[9]

Jesus made it clear that His "mother and brethren" were really those who were a part of His mission and ministry in the Kingdom of God, not just those of blood kin.[10] It is obvious that many of us have never learned the principle that we are brothers and sisters bought by a price,[11] and that price is the blood of Jesus Christ. It is that one blood that now brings us back into a new family relationship.[12]

It was no accident that Jesus Christ entered the human race with a skin color that was as close to the median between black and white as possible. According to Bible genealogy in Matthew 1:1-16 and Luke 3:23-38, Jesus was of Jewish origin. His skin color was neither black nor white. Again, this was no accident.

9.   Ephesians 4:25-32.
10.   Matthew 12:46-50.
11.   1 Corinthians 7:23.
12.   Galatians 4:5-7.

When I was a little boy, my daddy took me with him to a campground in Pennsylvania. I was allowed to go out with the boys and girls under a big tree where there was a Bible school for the kids. That's the first time I ever heard the little chorus, "Jesus Loves the Little Children." The verse goes, "Red and yellow, black and white, they are precious in His sight. Jesus loves the little children of the world."

Jesus is always trying to reach across to someone else. He reaches beyond every border to expand His Kingdom. He always goes to "the other side" to reach out to hurting people, demoniacs, and the lost. In the same way, He expects us to follow in His footsteps and cross over to "the other side" of our prejudices and fears. There are people who desperately need us, and we must cross over and minister to them.[13]

This is a touchy issue in modern Pentecostal and Charismatic circles, but we must never forget that God was striking down racial prejudice when He gave Peter a vision and forced him to "cross over" from a mere Hebrew concept of the Kingdom to the much broader base of a people of one blood as revealed in God's Word.[14]

Over and over again, we stubbornly return to fleshly racial divisions and prejudices that were totally and completely done away with by the gospel of the Lord Jesus Christ. It is now a gospel to "whosoever will." The "circumcision of the flesh" is no longer important, but it is through water baptism, which represents the circumcision of the heart, that we come into covenant with the Lord Jesus Christ.[15]

There seems to be a great need for more biblical study and understanding of the heart of God in the Church. We need to discern what the future holds in relationship to our being "one nation under God." Sometimes our excessive efforts to include a particular nation or people group that has been harmed or abused in the past simply fosters a continuation of their separation from our nation as a whole.

The Book of Revelation pictures a final day when people will be gathered together from every nation and every tongue.[16] If that is to be true in

---

13. Mark 4:35; 5:1-15.
14. Acts 10:9-16.
15. Romans 2:28-29; Colossians 2:11-12.
16. Revelation 7:9-10.

the eternities when Jesus Christ will come and rule and reign again, then why should it not begin to happen now?

This is not a day of reconciliation between the races; it is a day to recognize that in Christ we have been made to be new creatures.[17] In Christ, there is "neither bond nor free," and "there is neither male nor female."[18] You can properly add to this, "neither black nor white; neither rich nor poor." We are all one in the Lord Jesus Christ. The truth is (whether we like it or not), it is this conviction alone that can deal with the racial problems we will face in the future.

For many decades now, I have preached and predicted that the greatest battle of the future will take place between the "haves" and the "have nots." There is still a strong current of prejudice against indigents and those who are impoverished. Some people say, "Let them overcome their own poverty by the work of their own hands." They refuse to recognize that many of these people have been trapped in their environments, and that they have little or no chance of getting out unless someone from the outside crosses the line of risk and commitment to offer them help like a modern good Samaritan.

We are dealing with a much broader problem than just a "black and white" issue. We are dealing with a disease that divides the human race into so many divisive compartments that we will never be a true family of God unless we change. The Bride of Christ, I can promise you as a lifelong student of God's Word, will certainly not be made up of one nation, one race, or one kindred. It will be made up of all who have accepted the Lord Jesus Christ. Only in His name is there salvation, and there is salvation in none other.[19]

---

17. 2 Corinthians 5:17.
18. Galatians 3:28.
19. Acts 4:12.

A People Who Were Not

(Reba Rambo/Dony McGuire, New Kingdom Music/ASCAP ©1986. Used with permission.)

Sing those who were orphans, sing
Oh children of the promise, sing
We who were not heirs received adoption
We cry Abba Father, cry Abba Father

Sing those who were barren, sing
Travail in the Spirit, sing
'Cause our husband Christ, He claimed us with blood
Spiritual Israel, His Kingdom's born

We are that people who were not
God's peculiar people who were not
The seed of Abraham, Sons of God
A chosen generation, a witness for all the world to see
We are that people, we are the people of God.

Sing those who were barren, sing
Travail in the Spirit, sing
'Cause our husband Christ, He claimed His Bride with blood
Spiritual Israel, His Kingdom's born

We are that people who were not
God's peculiar people who were not
The seed of Abraham, Sons of God
A chosen generation, a witness for all the world to see
We are that people, we are the people of God.

We're not black or white,
We're not bond or free
We're no earthly race
We're a brand new breed.

We are that people
We are the people of God
We are that people
We are the people of God.

Chapter 5

The Statue of Liberty Speaks

Three hundred feet above the ocean on Ellis Island in New York City Harbor there stands a statue, its arms lifting a torch that beckons to all the world with this cry:

> Give me your tired, your poor,
> Your huddled masses yearning to be free,
> The wretched refuse of your teeming shore
> Send these, the homeless, tempest-tossed to me
> I lift my lamp beside the golden door!

The Statue of Liberty sends forth a call to mankind from all over the world. It stands as a symbol of hope to the disenfranchised and disadvantaged. Men and women from all around the globe have been invited to come to America if they are suffering from poverty, if life has been an experience of brokenness, or if all hope in their nation or environment offers nothing for the future.

People have come from all over the world in answer to this open invitation: men, women, and children looking for refuge and a place to begin life all over again. The people have been from all nationalities, from all races, and from every rank and income level around the world. Like no other nation on this planet, the United States is a true amalgamation of people from all nations and all races of the earth.

Could it be that God is using America as a test for the Kingdom of God? Is this land the site of a grand experiment to see if this is the time Jesus prayed about in chapter 17 of John? Of whom was Jesus praying when He cried, "Father, make them one"?

Too often we interpret this to mean our Lord was simply referring to His Church. I am sure there is an element of truth in this. The Lord wants the various parts of His Body to come together in unity so that the world may see a demonstration of togetherness.[1]

God always thinks of the earth as the place where His family dwells, because that was His original intent for this planet and for His people. Everything in the Bible record after the fall of mankind in the Book of Genesis is concerned with bringing this family back together into harmony, one with another and with God Himself. How did man get estranged from God in the first place? How did man begin to hate his brother so much that in the first family, Cain rose up in the field and killed Abel? Since the fall in the garden, man has been scattered all over the earth and often without purpose or design.

When God promised Abraham that He would make him a father of many nations in Genesis 17:4-5, this had little or nothing to do with "one" nation. Where else in the world could this concept be tested better than in the United States of America, where representatives of all nations now dwell? All of the world is very much aware that America is a "melting pot" for peoples from all nations and tribes of the earth.

God's hand has always been upon America because, from its birth, it has been very God-conscious. Although this has certainly changed in some ways in the past few years, we are still known around the world as a Christian nation. No other nation was birthed with such a high goal: to make all men equal and all men free. I believe without a doubt that the reason the things of God have been so viciously attacked in recent years is because of the great potential inherent in the future of America. If it is possible for harmony and unity to come to the human race in the United States of America, then it is somewhat symbolic of what the Kingdom of God will be like in its future dimension.

Why do men run such risks to reach the shores of the United States of America? Oppressed men and women come to this nation for its promise of security and freedom. When we hear the words "freedom, opportunity, and hope," we need to realize that they symbolize the answer to the problems of

---

1.   John 17:21-23.

hopeless people from all over the world. That explains the worldwide appreciation of the Statue of Liberty, which invites all to come who are poor, who are brokenhearted, and who are oppressed.

This invitation inscribed in the statue in New York City Harbor sounds very much like the words that Jesus spoke in the Gospel of Luke. He clearly said He had come to "preach the gospel to the poor."[2] This gospel wasn't given just to cause the poor man to "handle" or accept his poverty; it was a gospel of power providing the ways and means by which he could become prosperous and enjoy quality living.[3]

Jesus also said that He came "to heal [or mend] the brokenhearted."[4] Broken hearts around the world desperately need a place of healing. Countless numbers of innocent families and individuals have been trapped by political problems and strife that have forcibly divided their homes, and that have often brought death to members of their families. The brokenness of men and women around the world was of great concern to Jesus. He spoke of those who were oppressed, and today there are multitudes of people who are oppressed economically, socially, and politically in many nations in the earth.

The shores of the United States have traditionally welcomed people seeking refuge from an oppressive society. Jesus also spoke of those who were made captive. How many times have free men and women been taken captive and forced to serve as slaves to other people in various parts of the world? Lived out according to its constitution, the United States of America offers freedom to such captives.

Truly the household of faith is a peculiar people.[5] We know it is joined together by our common faith in the Lord Jesus Christ, but we often forget that its mission is to be salt and light to the nations of the earth![6] More than anywhere else in the world, the Church ought to be an influence in the United States, where all the nations are gathered.

2.   Luke 4:18.
3.   John 10:10b.
4.   Luke 4:18.
5.   1 Peter 2:9.
6.   Matthew 5:13-14.

If the unsaved citizens of the United States ever see true unity and body life in what we call the Church, then it is virtually certain that our country will also have a demonstration of what might take place among the nations of the earth. The Church is a picture in microcosm of how God wants the whole world to look. Remember, God so loved the world that He gave His only begotten Son.[7]

The Creator loved every nation, every race, and every tribe and tongue so much that He gave Himself in the Son to redeem us and make us one. We often think His love is "reserved" for the Church, but God wants to reconcile the whole world unto Himself.[8] This is what the gospel of the Kingdom is all about.

When the rule of Christ is practiced, men of all races and colors live together under the single command of the Lord Jesus Christ, the Lord of life and the Commander-in-chief. He is the Lord of His Church right now, but He is destined to be the Lord of all nations as well. Eventually, every knee will bow and every tongue will confess that He is Lord.[9]

The apostle John gave us a climactic picture of the human race in the Book of Revelation, in which he saw all the nations and tribes of the earth gathered together into one unit.[10] Isn't this the ultimate goal and purpose for which Jesus died? We know, of course, that not everyone will believe and receive Christ; however, that is our divine mission. Jesus commanded us to "preach the gospel to every creature."[11] The Master left no one out.

Where does this unity begin? It should begin in the Body of Christ, but something is awry in the Church. The American Church, and especially the Charismatic and Fundamental branches of the family, seems to be so caught up in its concern over the fulfillment of prophecy in national Israel that it has become deaf and blind to God's summons and movement to bring His people from all over the earth together into one great spiritual family.

---

7.   John 3:16.
8.   2 Corinthians 5:18-19.
9.   Philippians 2:9-11.
10.   Revelation 7:9-10.
11.   Mark 16:15.

The interpreters of last-day prophecies vary from one extreme to another, but honestly, what sign will truly proclaim the soon return of our Lord Jesus Christ? It is recorded in the Gospel of Matthew:

And when this gospel of the kingdom has been witnessed or demonstrated to the whole world, it is then that Christ will come again (Matthew 24:14, my paraphrase).

It is only when this rule of Christ has been demonstrated that Christ will return—regardless of what all the prophetic teachers may say. Our task is to bring about a mature Body of Christ that will be an example of unity to the whole world.

No one appreciates more than I the important place of the nation of Israel in prophecy. I fully appreciate what the Jewish people have done in the past to bring about God's will for mankind. There is little doubt in my mind that this great nation has a crucial place in prophecy. I fear, however, that we have overlooked many signs pointing to the coming of Jesus that have nothing to do with what happens to natural Israel.

Yet an even more important question looms in my mind: "What must the blood-washed Church do to hasten the coming of the Lord?" The answer, again, comes from our Lord's lips. We must answer the prayer that Jesus so fervently prayed, "Father, make them one so the world may know...."[12] The Church was divinely commissioned to be salt and light to the world.[13] It is the fulfillment of this commission that will hasten the return of Jesus!

Despite the unavoidable clarity of this truth, Sunday morning remains the most segregated hour of the week in America! This was one of Martin Luther King, Jr.'s greatest concerns. He often remarked as we talked in small informal groups, "Something has to take place that will cause the Church to be more aware of how we can somehow tear down the prejudice that still remains in our churches!"

Segregation doesn't peak during the working hours, or in the workplace, or in athletic functions. Christians would like to see this issue go away, but sooner or later we will have to tear down the walls between the races if we ever want to have a true family of God.

12. John 17:21-23.
13. Matthew 5:13-14.

We will miss the mark as long as we spend the majority of our time and energy trying to "find our roots" or deciding which nation God is "blessing the most." As long as these things dominate our priorities, we will never see that "chosen people" arise who trace their origin to the blood of Jesus Christ, not to some fallen past in the flesh.

The blunt truth is that God is far more concerned about our fruits than about our roots.[14] Once we come to the Lord Jesus Christ, we are not the same as we were in the past anyway! Now all things have become new, and we are now a new creation in Christ.[15] As new creations in Christ, in His eyes we are neither bond nor free, male nor female, or haves or have nots— we are all one in the Lord Jesus Christ.[16]

I wrote this chapter while en route to Miami, Florida, from Atlanta. We were on a mission to "adopt" another public housing development and bring hope to the residents there who felt trapped by their environment. Fifty teenagers from our church were already working in the housing projects, speaking to teenage residents there about Jesus Christ. They were giving each one of them a Bible and inviting them to a pizza party where we would have an opportunity to give them hope in Christ and build relationships.

We were working through Pastor Wayne Cochran, the pastor of the Voice of Jesus Christian Center in Miami, who was networking with us. His teenagers and worship teams were set to participate with our people in a celebration that would include a formal "adoption" of the housing community by the Voice of Jesus Christian Center. This would help establish and develop genuine relationships in the housing community.

This ministry was part of a program we call "Operation Dignity," which we established to give dignity to every human being. Jesus said that He had come "that He might give life and give it more abundantly."[17] For this reason, we developed this ministry program to help bring people to a higher level of living.

On my way home from that celebration service in the Miami housing projects, I jotted down a brief account of the results. I had been taken directly

14. Titus 3:8-9.
15. 2 Corinthians 5:16-18.
16. Galatians 3:28.
17. See John 10:10b.

to the housing development, and I was thrilled to see how many people had gathered to experience this developing relationship between that local church, the families living in the development, and various government agencies.

We met with commissioners from Dade County, Florida, and learned they were delighted that we had come to the area to help the housing community. In fact, the Housing Authority even gave their official approval and a great deal of assistance to our efforts, particularly the resident managers and local officials. It was a joy to see such a joint effort by so many factions of society to help a community in need.

Our program was designed to bring literacy programs, scouting programs, tutorial programs, personal health and hygiene programs, and programs teaching job search and interview skills to the residents, all at no cost to them.

I was especially happy to hear that many young people were won to the Lord Jesus Christ, and three adult block captains also accepted Christ as Lord and Savior. I was deeply impressed with a comment made by one of the commissioners to Pastor Wayne Cochran and myself. He said, "Force us, as elected officials, to help you in these projects that you are undertaking!"

It says a lot when a government official asks us to be salt and light, the very influence God has called us to become to the world. I have to say that none of this was new to me, however. From our earliest days at Chapel Hill Harvester Church, we have reached out in practical ways to the urban poor of Atlanta, regardless of the color of their skin.

When we adopted Bankhead Courts (a housing project in Metro Atlanta), it had the reputation of being one of the city's most dangerous and drug-infested neighborhoods. According to police records at that time, officers were called to that 500-apartment complex more than ten times a day! Things were so bad in December of 1988 that for a three-day period, the U.S. Postal Service suspended all deliveries to the housing project because of the outbreak of violence there. Well-meaning politicians and community activists had been literally run out of the complex, and many simply gave up hope of ever changing the situation.

Nevertheless, we decided to adopt the 1,700 residents of Bankhead. In May of 1989, we held a rally in the neighborhood with messages by the pastors and performances by the choir, a vocal ensemble, and our orchestra.

We also featured contemporary Christian music, and our arts department performed their live production of "Broadway Night."

For black youngsters whose only role models had been diamond-studded drug lords in the projects, our musicians, especially those who were black, represented a fresh alternative for imitation. When our teachers began visiting regularly to give the children lessons in voice, dance, drama, reading, sewing, drawing, makeup techniques, fashion design, and even rap music, the results were astonishing.

Scores of formerly shy children began to come out of their shells. Some of them even adopted the first names of our instructors as nicknames for themselves. Those kids formed a choir, and learned choreographed songs of hope written by our composer, Anthony Lockett. They even managed to win first place among 43 contestants in three categories at the annual Atlanta Housing Project Talent Show! (Never before had their neighborhood won a single prize in the competition.)

We saw the confidence and self-esteem of those children soar as they learned to express themselves in the fine arts. They performed at our church, for City Housing Authority officials in Atlanta, and even at a city-wide anti-drug rally. We learned that educators at the local public schools serving those projects began to notice a difference in the academic performance of these youths. The entire atmosphere of the complex changed so much that the crime rates dropped for the entire area! As one young girl put it: "Ever since you people came from the church, I'm not afraid anymore." Best of all, children at Bankhead were coming to the Lord. In one rap session alone, 18 teenagers became Christians.

You need to know that Operation Dignity began in the heart of one young woman, Patti Battle. After I preached a sermon calling for action in the inner-city housing projects, Patti asked me, "When is the church going to do something?" I answered, "When are YOU going to do something?" She took my question to heart and started to make a difference by personally visiting Bankhead Courts and by developing a relationship with the Tenants' Association. Then she met with the proper authorities and asked for permission to have a "birthday club" for the children. Little by little, Patti recruited workers to help, and gradually added more and more programs to change the quality of life for these people.

The Housing Authority was so impressed that they gave Patti and the church an apartment unit as a permanent headquarters. They also invited us to begin similar programs at other housing projects, and now we are ministering at Atlanta's East Lake Meadows and Boatrock Housing Projects, in addition to Bankhead Courts.

Former Atlanta Mayor Maynard Jackson asked us to host a conference so other churches could learn from our experience. In 1990, Atlanta's chief of police, Eldrin Bell, testified to a "U.S. congressional subcommittee and referred to our ministry and the residents of the Bankhead Housing Projects. He said the Bankhead success "was an example of what could happen when a certain church gets involved," and that "such projects are worthy and deserve federal support."

Finally, our Operation Dignity program was awarded a "Point of Light" by President Bush as being "one of the most effective in the area of joining together the private sector with the government" to try to help families who are in such great need.

Is there hope in America? If there is hope, it must come through the Church. We are all well aware of the countless failures of the government and its welfare programs, educational endeavors, and many other man-centered programs that we now know cannot last. When the Church is mature, when it accepts the responsibility to take care of the little ones, of the aged, and of all those who fall under our care, then we will begin to see progress.

As the Church grows in its maturity and solves the racial problem, the people of America will realize that something special has taken place. Will we, the Church, fail the test, or will we press on and accomplish what God has intended for us? Will we pay the price to be a proper influence and bring together the various peoples of the earth? Perhaps we should realize that since this was the cry and the prayer of Jesus Christ Himself, then it ought to be our chief concern as well!

The Multitudes

(Anthony Lockett, Cathedral Praise Publ. ©1989. Used with permission.)

There's a multitude living in the streets
Without a place to sleep, no food to eat
There's a multitude trapped by poverty,
No faith to believe they can be free.
There's a multitude of homes falling apart,
Single parents raising children with wounded hearts.
There's a multitude of children in homes left all alone,
No parents to call their own.

CHORUS:
We must feed them by meeting their needs;
We must show them with action and deeds;
We must give them the hope for a better life
And restore them to the fullness of Christ.

There's a multitude of the elderly
Kept by strangers, left by their own.
There's a multitude with infirmities,
Searching for a cure to be made whole.
There's a multitude of people everywhere,
The body of believers sharing the love of God
There's a multitude willing to obey,
Marching to triumph with a healing rod.

Chapter 6

The Sound of Unity

The year was 1983. A young girl was playing with dolls, unaware that she was being observed. After a time, she separated the dolls according to the color of their skin, and then the dolls began to fight. The drama continued to play out as the young girl went through the painful process of growth and maturation until finally she prepared for her wedding, as a bride ready for union with her groom. Grown, adorned, without spot or wrinkle, the Bride of Christ, the Church, had come of age.[1]

I have just described a scene from a musical drama called "The Bride," written by Gary Thurman, a young man who was raised in our church. After the first production of "The Bride" at our church, two talented composers and members of the church, Dony and Reba McGuire, were inspired to write an original musical score for the drama. The complete musical drama has since been performed around the world, but nowhere was the performance so powerful as in strife-torn South Africa, before the plague of apartheid had been struck down.

Neville and Wendy McDonald, the pastors of Good Hope Christian Center in Constantia, South Africa, performed the drama in a large rented stadium in Durban. It was such a hit that they had to run the production a number of times to accommodate the people who were waiting in long lines to purchase tickets.

The production had such an impact in South Africa that thousands of miles and a whole world away, *The Wall Street Journal* printed an astounding statement about the Durban phenomenon:

---

1. Ephesians 5:27; Revelation 19:7.

"Kingdom theology first entered South Africa four years ago when a drama written by Mr. Paulk's church, was performed at a church in Durban. The spirit motivating these charismatics may be the best, if not the only, path to the elusive goal of racial justice without bloodshed in South Africa."

I was later asked by government officials in South Africa to write down my suggestions for solutions to the race problems in South Africa. They promptly submitted my suggestions directly to President DeKlerk. I believe parts of those ideas were folded into some of DeKlerk's thinking as he began to make moves to turn over the government to Mandela. South Africa faced one of the same problems we faced here in the South—people had developed deep-seated and erroneous convictions about race relations basically because they heard it taught from the Bible.

It has been said that the South African system of apartheid (which was simply their written version of what we would call Jim Crow laws) was established after an address before that nation's legislators by a preacher who used the Bible to justify racism toward non-whites. "The Bride" confronted this untruth using the creative arts to communicate to both the heart and the soul.

I believe there is great truth in the saying, "Music is the universal language." One of the most important things the Church must address is its music. Our music must transcend any particular race, culture, or background, because worship is the force that makes people feel one in the house of God.

We had already moved from downtown Atlanta to South DeKalb County when the choir became integrated in the 1970's, but it took a little longer for our music to be integrated as well. One day, some of the choir members went to Clariece, who is our Minister of Music, and asked her if they could have a talent show. She immediately approved of their idea, but she was very surprised the night of the production because the new black choir members had formed a singing group as one of the acts.

Clariece was so delighted with their sound that she asked them to sing in a church service. Clariece had recorded with black musicians many times before she was married, but up until that point, there had not been enough black singers to try black gospel music in our church.

The first song they sang was so appropriate: "I Can't Stop Praising His Name...Jesus." It was Palm Sunday, and when I began to preach about the triumphant Christ, the group struck up that triumphant chorus again. Each time I continued the sermon, they would begin again…"I can't stop praising His name." A new level of worship was reached that day.

The new black ensemble was formally named "The Hallelujah Chorus," and they began to rehearse on Tuesday evenings while the full church choir rehearsed on Thursday evenings. (The members of the ensemble attended both rehearsals.) Before long, a number of other choir members began to stand up and sing along with "The Hallelujah Chorus."

Clariece finally said, "We're not going to have a black choir, and we're not going to have a white choir. We're all going to sing together. In fact, we're going to sing all kinds of music, and we're going to rehearse together on the same night!"

Her premise was that when we get to Heaven, we're not going to have individual corners for each race of people to sing their own songs. We will all be praising God together around the throne, so we might as well get started now.

Just as my sister-in-law expected, her progress toward musical integration wasn't entirely smooth or totally welcomed by our church family. I have seen the process take place again and again. I cannot tell you how many times some of our white parishioners said to me or to our worship leaders, "I just don't know how to move with black gospel music." The same thing happened when we featured some great hymns of the Church, or some of the other types of music. Sure enough, a few of the black believers in our family would say, "Well, I'm not sure that I can relate to this form of music."

But on the other hand, there is a danger in stereotyping someone. Today, our black members enjoy the symphony just as much as the white people, and most of our white members genuinely enjoy gospel music. Again, the problem is this: "We don't know what we like—we like what we know." The Church has a divine call and mandate to break down these walls of division and to make "God's music" in God's house. We are to sing a new song, to offer up something fresh and new every day! Maybe God is trying to bring a new sound to His people that will be difficult for anyone to stereotype or label with any racial background.

Clariece often makes another powerful and even prophetic statement about worship: "We must take the excellence portrayed in the world of arts and entertainment, the liturgy and reverence of the high church, the joy and uninhibited praise of the black tradition, and the natural, God-given talent in the Pentecostal churches, and combine them in order to present to God a glorious worship, worthy of His majesty."

Certain forms, traditions, and methodologies from our various denominational backgrounds still separate us. Some of us favor what might be called "Episcopal" forms of government, while others prefer congregational government structures or some other structure. There is no great tragedy in churches adopting various forms and methods of operation. However, we must never allow these things to separate us from other members of the Body of Christ! We need to "rightly discern" the truth that we all belong to one big family of God, born of one blood. The apostle Paul told us how to relate to one another in his Epistle to the Corinthians:

> *For as the body is one, and hath many members, and all the members of that one body, being many, are one body: so also is Christ. For by one Spirit are we all baptized into one body, whether we be Jews or Gentiles, whether we be bond or free; and have been all made to drink into one Spirit. For the body is not one member, but many. If the foot shall say, Because I am not the hand, I am not of the body; is it therefore not of the body? And if the ear shall say, Because I am not the eye, I am not of the body; is it therefore not of the body?* (1 Corinthians 12:12-16)

When the apostle Paul found himself in Athens, Greece, among Athenians and foreigners from many nations around the world, he presented a formal argument for his faith at the Acropolis on what was called Mars Hill.[2] Paul observed that the Athenians had erected an idol to "the unknown God," and he boldly proceeded to declare more about this God to his multinational, cross-cultural, non-Jewish audience. This is part of his message:

> *God, who made the world and everything in it, since He is Lord of heaven and earth, does not dwell in temples made with hands. Nor is He worshiped with men's hands, as though He needed anything, since He gives to all life, breath, and all things. And He*

---

2.   Acts 17:21-22.

hath made from one blood every nation of men to dwell on all the
face of the earth, and has determined their preappointed times
and the boundaries of their habitation, so that they should seek
the Lord, in the hope that they might grope for Him and find Him,
though He is not far from each one of us; for in Him we live and
move and have our being, as also some of your own poets have
said, "For we are also His offspring" (Acts 17:24-28 NKJV).

The apostle Paul boldly told his international audience that they were all of "one blood." Many have argued that when this verse speaks of having set our "habitation," it is referring to racial separation. But it is obvious that Paul was not talking about national boundary lines or racial division, but rather describing the limitation of the human race and the pre-appointed times of God. Regardless, the point the apostle Paul was making here was that God created all men on an equal basis, regardless of race, and that all people had one origin!

If we ever hope to make any headway in tearing down these walls separating mankind by color and nationality, then we must begin by making certain quality decisions about our relationships and actions.

First, we need to rediscover the biblical mandate that mankind is descended from a single origin.[3] Few Bible-believing Christians would doubt the fact that we are all descendants of Adam and Eve. If this is so, then from a natural point of view, we are of one blood. Many ask, "Why, then, did all the various skin colors and races develop?" The Bible record makes it obvious that this took place because of the rebellion at the tower of Babel. It was here that God scattered people in all directions after confusing their tongues. Obviously, various races and colors began to surface in different parts of the earth.[4]

Only outright ignorance can explain why someone would say the separation of mankind into diverse races and tongues at Babel was "God's original plan for mankind"! On the contrary, man's separation was the evil fruit of his prideful attempt to "become a god unto himself" in direct rebellion against and in rejection of God. The only logical path is to begin with the

3.   Genesis 3:20.
4.   Genesis 11:1-9.

premise that God's original intention was to have one family with a common heritage, and equal status as beloved children in His presence.

The second step is to understand that God called Abraham as an instrument to bring back together again and to transform His dispersed family of man into what might be called a "family of faith." He promised Abraham that his seed would be like the stars of the skies and the sands of the sea, and would include people from all the nations of the earth.[5] Obviously, God was reversing what had taken place at Babel!

It was going to take some time for this promise to be fulfilled—it only reached its fruition at the birth of Jesus Christ, who is called the "seed of Abraham" in Galatians 3:16. Rebellion was reversed by the obedience of Jesus Christ,[6] who was both the Son of God and the son of Abraham.

The third step then is to proclaim our oneness in Jesus Christ. Through His shed blood, we now have a common heritage. Old things, even our natural roots and cultural background, are now washed away and we become one in the Lord Jesus Christ. Once this takes place, we are bound only by the instructions in the New Testament, which restricts our social relationships only as it has to do with unbelievers. Paul made it abundantly clear that we were not to be unequally yoked with unbelievers.[7] This passage has nothing to do with nationality.

Finally, we need an experience of the heart, a visitation from God to settle the matter so we know there is absolutely no place for racial prejudices in the Body of Christ. It is important to remember that according to the New Testament, there is no "chosen race" in natural terms that has been selected and empowered by God to rule over other nations. We are under the Lordship of Jesus Christ and are all on a very level playing field. We are to bow before Jesus Christ alone, and no other.[8]

Once we have this experience of heart and know that we are indeed one family under God, then we must take down the walls that have separated us for so many years, beginning with the area of relationships. Here again, Martin Luther King, Jr., made it clear that his greatest concern was having proper relationships between all races under God. True to his

5. Genesis 22:17-18; Romans 4:16-17.
6. Hebrews 5:8-9.
7. 2 Corinthians 6:14.
8. Luke 22:25-26; 1 Peter 5:1-4.

biblical foundation, he never suggested that one race should dominate over another.

We must develop proper, godly relationships in every area, including our social activities. In any area of society, even in the church, it is all too common to see various races yield to the tendency to move toward those of their own kind, or their own race, or color when socializing.

In recent years, an erroneous theme has crept into many of the Pentecostal and Charismatic circles as some preachers have declared from the pulpit that one race is superior to another. This is inappropriate, and in a very real sense, anti-Christ.

This kind of hate-mongering enabled Adolph Hitler to separate and finally destroy the nation of Germany while negatively affecting the entire world. He tried to prove that there was a superior race, and used his platform of race hatred to murder millions of innocent people while destroying his own nation.

Now we hear some black preachers boldly declaring that it is time for the black race to come forward and "be the superior race that God intended it to be." This kind of message will only separate the Body of Christ. The Bible has the final word on this matter. It declares that the time has come when we must recognize that we are all on an equal basis under the Lordship of Jesus Christ.

As I mentioned earlier, it is extremely dangerous for us to stereotype people according to their race or color. There are all sorts of talents and gifts among all races of people. As long as we think that black people are particularly gifted in music or singing (but in no other area), we have made a grave error. When we believe that "only black people" can move with certain dramatic gestures, or spontaneous dancing, then again we have made a grave error.

In the same way, it is wrong to assume that only white people should embrace more stoic forms of worship. No single form of worship or music is "approved" to the exclusion of others, according to the Word of the Lord. God is seeking those who will "worship Him in spirit and in truth."[9]

The Bible provides many examples of ways we can open ourselves up to worship and praise before God. Sometimes it is through the playing of

9.   John 4:23-24.

instruments, and at other times it may be through different forms of bowing before the Lord or through songs and hymns.[10] The Word of the Lord clearly speaks of dancing before the Lord in Psalm 149:3. All of these can lead us into a fresh experience with God.

I believe it is extremely important that we begin to open our eyes to the new leadership God will use to minister to the members of His family in fresh ways and to make them one. Don't look at the color of someone who becomes a leader, just as you wouldn't look at his or her toes or larynx as criterion of eligibility! Stop making statements such as, "Well, I am going to a black church because I want to be under black leadership," or "I am going to a white church because I want to be under white leadership." God chooses and anoints leaders for the entire Body of Christ, not for just one particular race.

The Church must stand as one family and one body comprised of many individual members. It is only through this kind of unity that we can have the power of influence that God intended us to have. We must unite into a strong force to be the salt and light in the world that God desires. Few people are going to listen to one little church in a rented storefront location, even if there is a title on the door that says "a bishop preaches here."

On the other hand, any church that is making a difference in the world and bringing solutions to society can't help but influence government! Numbers count for political power and clout, and these things are necessary sometimes to change the environment in which we live. When the Church truly becomes one, we will be able to speak to government and have a strong influence in areas such as public housing, welfare, health programs, public education, or any other area of grave concern.

One of our top priorities in the Church today should be the training of our young people. Young people who grow up with the same prejudices we experienced in life may never make progress in bringing to pass the rule of Christ. We must begin in our church-sponsored schools, where we are free to train boys and girls to think as God would have them think.

It is ludicrous to believe that we can allow atheists and unbelievers to teach our children six and eight hours a day, and then expect them to be devoted Christians. This would be like turning over the children of the Israelites

---

10.   Psalm 95:6; 150:4; Colossians 3:16.

to the Philistines every day to teach them the ways of the Philistines. It is time now for us to get serious about Christian education.

We are entering a very "enlightened" age when educational tools are virtually unlimited. We can now "see the world" from our homes, and can even "speak" to the world on some of the new computerized methods such as the Internet. In light of this new technology, the young people we are raising today will be living in "one world" indeed, where communication around the globe to a person in a different culture will be just as effortless as a call across the street to a neighbor!

Obviously Wendell Wilkie was far ahead of his time many decades ago when he ran for President and spoke about this being "one world." The world is growing smaller and smaller and national boundary lines are no longer holding up under the pressure of global economics and cultural interchange. With modern communication systems and state-of-the-art digital satellites circling the globe, there is no way to force people to see themselves as citizens of one nation instead of being a part of a truly international scene. The days of isolation are over, thanks to the tremendous speed of transportation and the incredible communication tools now at our disposal.

Boys and girls growing up today must learn that this is, in fact, one earth; and the earth belongs to the Lord.[11] Of course I understand that the world systems dominating our world today are merely temporal things that are passing away.[12] But rest assured, the earth is like the heavens. They will be renewed and will not pass away, according to the Word of the Lord in the writing of the apostle Peter. Indeed, they will be purged, but they will not pass away. They will simply become something new.[13] If, in fact, we are looking for solutions to the problems on this planet, the best place to begin is by properly teaching the ways of God to our boys and girls.

Hear me very clearly when I tell you, "We must reevaluate those whom God has blessed." I hear church leaders and believers saying over and over again, "We must bless the Israelites and we must be constantly praying over Jerusalem." Again, I pray that you do not misunderstand what I am saying. The words I am hearing are not the words of Jesus to the

---

11. Psalm 24:1.
12. 1 John 2:16-17.
13. 2 Peter 3:13.

Church. Jesus clearly told us who was blessed in His eyes. Hear Him again as He proclaims from the ancient Book of Isaiah:

> *Blessed are the poor in spirit, for theirs is the kingdom of heaven. Blessed are those who mourn, for they shall be comforted. Blessed are the meek, for they shall inherit the earth. Blessed are those who hunger and thirst for righteousness, for they shall be filled. Blessed are the merciful, for they shall obtain mercy. Blessed are the pure in heart, for they shall see God. Blessed are the peacemakers, for they shall be called sons of God. Blessed are those who are persecuted for righteousness' sake, for theirs is the kingdom of heaven* (Matthew 5:3-10 NKJV).

These are the ones who are blessed. These are the people God lifts up today. Frankly, it is very difficult for me to believe that God's blessings rest upon anyone who tramples underfoot the blood of Jesus Christ, regardless of his race or national origin. The Word makes it abundantly clear that Jesus Christ is not only the chief cornerstone, but also the stumbling block.[14] Some people don't understand that God is moving on today, with a new blessed people who are under His anointing, and who are changing the world as they preach and teach the gospel of the Kingdom as Jesus did before them.

There was a time when God winked at our ignorance and overlooked our lack of knowledge, according to Acts 17:30. But be it known that from the lack of knowledge, the people perish.[15] The time has come for us to address those issues that are important to God.

The blessings of God today abundantly rest upon those who are in covenant with Him.[16] These people have not only been baptized and experienced the circumcision of their hearts, but have also dined at His table. They have eaten of His flesh and received the cup of His blood, and have experienced the genuine presence of Christ.

It is more and more obvious to us that those who are firstfruit (ten percent or tithe) givers according to Proverbs 3:9-10, along with those who add

---

14. 1 Peter 2:6-8.
15. Hosea 4:6.
16. Exodus 19:5-6.

the offerings described in Malachi 3:8, are blessed people. They joyfully provide the earthly ways and means of sowing seed and reaping harvest. These people are blessed of the Lord.[17]

I believe God is looking for a Church today upon which He can pour out unlimited blessings! It will be a Church that is absolutely purged of its racial differences, and can sit at the feet of Jesus in unity as the family of God. Then we will see how much we need the various nationalities that make up the beautiful family of God. That Church will have no envy or jockeying for position. The total and complete cooperation of its members in a spirit of unity will, in fact, hasten the coming of our Lord.

When Jesus shall come again "in the clouds with great power and glory," and "every eye shall see Him," and we shall all hear those words, "Time [is] no longer,"[18] I believe Jesus will come for a Church and Bride that has broken down these walls of separation. Now is the time to lay down our private agendas and attend to the priorities of God.

The Church of the twenty-first century must be a Church such as we have not seen before. I call it the "eleventh hour Church," and the eleventh hour generation.[19] Many were sent into the harvest at various times of the day, but now we have come to the closing of the hour. Those who enter the harvest field today must be ready to work rapidly and efficiently. This cannot be done by laborers whose hearts are filled with fear, bitterness, or prejudice. God will only work with those whose hearts do not condemn them.

I believe the power of prayer is one of the most important things the New Testament Church must address in the twenty-first century. We have seen a tremendous revival in relationships in recent months wherever people were teaching about prayer. I believe that God raised up Larry Lea a number of years ago to call the Church to prayer. Although he has undergone great battles in his ministry, he has now overcome the obstacles and adversity to continue the work God called him to do. Larry Lea was not called simply to build up intercessors in a local church; he was commissioned to deliver a "wake-up" call to be heard and heeded by the entire Church: "Seek the face of God!"

17. Malachi 3:10-11.
18. Mark 13:26; Revelation 1:7; 10:6.
19. Matthew 20:6-7.

I was excited to learn that even scientific research has proven that the power of prayer affects our physical bodies in a very positive way. This is but a stepping stone to our dream of loosing the force of prayer to stop violence in the streets and to turn nations away from the weapons of warfare and toward the peace that can come only from God.

The Lord's return cannot take place as long as we permit obstacles to separate us into nationalities with racial differences. He will come only when there is one body with a single heart and a single mind that truly reflects Jesus Christ to the world. This is the Church that I believe will be successful in the twenty-first century.

We Are the People of God

(Anthony Lockett, Cathedral Praise Publ. ©1989. Used with permission.)

We're an army unified by the blood.
We march in ranks distributing love.
Our defense is our covenant we have with the Father and the Son of man.
Though we have a foe—we're dressed for war,
The Holy Ghost is our force.
We've got generals all across the globe
Teaching the ways of God and restoring lost souls.

We are the people of God taking orders from the Father—in unity.
We are the people of God with the power to devour—the enemy.
We are the people of God purchased with the blood of Jesus—at Calvary.
We are the people of God speaking with tongues as we march on to victory.

We are the salt of the earth giving light to a hopeless world.
We've been given divine instructions to heal the brokenhearted, to set the
    captive free.
When the Word of God is spoken we anoint our ears to hear by the Spirit
    in godly fear.
The orders are clear—destroy the works of Satan,
And every evil thing that keeps people in chains.

We are the people of God taking orders from the Father in unity.
We are the people of God loving others as our brother in harmony.
We are the people of God with the power to devour the enemy.
We are the people of God, we're a new breed of Abraham's seed; we've
    got the keys.

The Church of today will either be triumphant or it will be trampled by
    the forces of Satan.
Jesus said, "The gates of hell shall not prevail against My Church."
What do you say? I say that we have the power to accomplish the task that
    God has assigned to us.
You ask me how we can do it?
We're gonna do it by being obedient to God and by being aggressive
    against Satan.

You and I together can overcome him.
This is the day of the Church.

When the Word of God is spoken we anoint our ears to hear
By the Spirit in godly fear.
The orders are clear—destroy the works of Satan,
And every evil thing that keeps people in chains.

We are the people of God purchased with the blood of Jesus at Calvary.
We are the people of God speaking with tongues as we march on to victory.
We are the people of God with the power to devour the enemy.
We are the people of God, we're a new breed of Abraham's seed; we've
    got the keys.

This picture of a little girl holding a placard during a civil rights protest in the South speaks volumes about the importance of teaching our children what God says about race relations and respect for all people created in His image. (Copyright © Michael Dwyer.)

Dr. Martin Luther King, Jr., delivered many of his most powerful addresses from behind a pulpit, and in the shadow of a cross. He delivered this message from a church pulpit in Selma, Alabama, in 1965 in his capacity as the chairman of the Southern Christian Leadership Conference. (Copyright © Archive Photos, 1994.)

Nonviolent black and white civil rights demonstrators are confronted by a line of policemen with helmets and nightsticks in Selma, Alabama. Although the marchers, led by Dr. Martin Luther King, Jr., gave no provocation, they were later assaulted with billy clubs, fire hoses, and attack dogs, which captured the attention of the nation and the White House. (Copyright © Archive Photos, 1995.)

When violence struck the peaceful civil rights marchers in Selma, Alabama, scenes like this one involving whites and blacks helping one another, became commonplace. (Copyright © Archive Photos, 1995.)

The power of Dr. Martin Luther King, Jr.'s nonviolent message of racial equality under God was its simplicity and its spiritual foundations. "Dr. King was a great preacher first and always," Bishop Paulk recalls. "His convictions stemmed directly from his deep faith in God and his understanding of the Scriptures." (Copyright © Archive Photos, 1996.)

Mrs. Coretta Scott King, flanked by her son, Dexter, the Rev. Jesse Jackson (left), and Ralph D. Abernathy, mourn the assassination of Dr. Martin Luther King, Jr., in Memphis, Tennessee, as the nation looks on. Mr. Abernathy assumed the chairmanship of the Southern Christian Leadership Conference after Dr. King's death. (Copyright © Steve Shapiro.)

Early in his career, a young Pentecostal preacher named Earl Paulk sent this picture home to "Mama," who was always one of his biggest supporters and a faithful "prayer warrior."

Newlyweds, Norma (Davis) and Earl Paulk met while studying at Furman University in Greenville, South Carolina. After graduation, they worked together in Sunday school and youth leadership in Georgia.

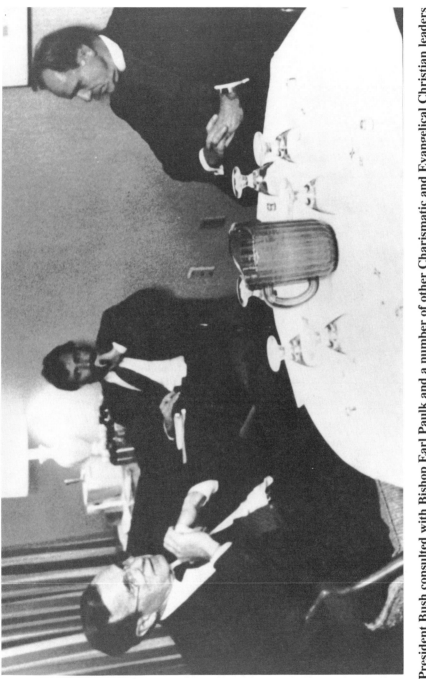

President Bush consulted with Bishop Earl Paulk and a number of other Charismatic and Evangelical Christian leaders during his tenure in the White House. The talks focused on a number of issues, including racial harmony, family values, and morality and ethics.

One of the keys to successful ministry in a congregation of "one blood" is to genuinely "love the sheep" regardless of race, color, culture, or gender. Bishop Earl Paulk's ministry has been built on a simple, consistent, Christlike love for the sheep placed in his care by God.

The Rev. Jesse Jackson speaks to the congregation of Chapel Hill Harvester Church. Many of America's most prominent black leaders have come to Chapel Hill to see the miracle of a church of "one blood" gathered together under the banner of Christ's love.

The congregation of Chapel Hill Harvester Church was asked to represent the fulfillment of the late Dr. Martin Luther King, Jr.'s dream of true integration of the races under God during the Martin Luther King, Jr., Parade held in Atlanta, Georgia, to mark his birthday. It was the only racially integrated float to appear in the parade, which received international news coverage.

Bishop Earl Paulk, accompanied by Yolanda King, addresses the crowd during the Kingfest Arts Festival, held each year in Atlanta. Musicians, artists, and performers from Chapel Hill Harvester Church regularly represent the Lord and their congregation at this nationally recognized arts festival.

Pastor John Garlington was a man "sent from God" to deliver a ringing prophecy to Bishop Earl Paulk and the entire congregation of Chapel Hill Harvester Church. His prophecy, reproduced in its entirety in the text of this book, has been proven to be miraculously accurate and true.

Bishop Earl Paulk addresses a predominantly black crowd at the first meeting held at Bankhead Courts, then one of Atlanta's most notorious inner city public housing projects. This was just the first of many highly effective outreaches to Bankhead residents, and later on, to residents in other public housing developments around the United States.

The Cathedral Choir, the racially integrated music ministry team from Chapel Hill Harvester Church and the Cathedral of the Holy Spirit, ministers to the public from the steps of the King Center in Atlanta, Georgia.

Christian television personality and leader Ben Kinchlow joins Bishop Earl Paulk in a fervent prayer for unity among the races.

Seven bishops of the International Charismatic College of Bishops gathered together for a time of prayer, consultation, and ministry. From left are Bishops Blair, McAlister, Paulk, Idahosa, Tito, Meares, and Mushegan.

Christian recording artists Donnie McClurkin (left) and Cindy Hall sing an anointed duet entitled, "More Than Wonderful," as the congregation members of Chapel Hill Harvester Church rise to their feet.

Bishop Earl Paulk concludes a joint concert by his sister-in-law, Clariece Paulk, and celebrated Christian recording artist Richard Smallwood. Dynamic music ministry has become a hallmark of Chapel Hill Harvester Church, and it spans a wide range of music tastes and formats: from classical orchestra performances to soul, and from rhythm and blues to Christian alternative rock.

"Jesus" (played by the son-in-law of Hosea Williams) stands before His accusers in a performance during the National Black Arts Festival held at Chapel Hill Harvester Church. This is but one of the many ways the local congregation opens its doors and heart to the greater Atlanta community in the name of Christ.

The children of Chapel Hill Harvester Church have become a living picture and demonstration of Dr. Martin Luther King, Jr.'s dream of "white children and black children" living together in unity and love.

Archbishop Benson Idahosa of Uganda declares in prayer on bended knee, "Behold, it is done!" in an unforgettable meeting of believers of many races and cultures in the Cathedral of the Holy Spirit.

Andrew Young, former U.N. Ambassador and Mayor of Atlanta, right, flanked by Bishop Earl Paulk, made a special appearance at Chapel Hill Harvester Church to personally announce the selection of Atlanta, Georgia, as the host city for the 1996 Olympic Games.

Chapter 7

The Pentecostal and the Collar

I can still hear myself saying, "Any man who wears his collar backwards obviously does not know what direction he is going!" As a young Pentecostal preacher, I had quickly learned that this time-tested phrase would always arouse a camp meeting crowd and spark a hearty chorus of "Amens" and loud shouts of approval. It was strictly a prejudiced religious statement of course, and in later years I was to be corrected by the Holy Spirit for embracing it so blindly.

The sad fact is that today there is probably more prejudice among religions than between races! If we stop for a moment and are honest with ourselves, we have to acknowledge that many of the wars of the past have had religious origins. The same is true of the more recent conflicts in Bosnia, and of course, in Ireland and Lebanon. No one can deny that the many battles over Jerusalem between the Arabs and the Jews have filled the front pages of our daily newspapers for years. Excessive competition and erroneous convictions have caused many people to act in very irresponsible and deadly ways.

By the time we had reached the early 1980's, I had been involved in the racial struggle for many years and was finally enjoying some of its more positive benefits. I was proud to be able to say that I was a part of the Civil Rights Movement as a very active minister involved in correcting social wrongs, particularly here in the South. I didn't realize that God had another prejudice in His sights.

I remember the day I was driving down a street near inner-city Atlanta. I was rejoicing over how much progress we had made in our local church concerning the racial problem. The church was very much integrated, and it seemed we had won this battle. I was very proud to think of how far we had come in the last few years, having raised up Atlanta's first multiracial integrated church despite seemingly impossible circumstances.

Then I saw a young Roman Catholic priest standing by the side of the road waiting to get on a bus. I noticed he was wearing his clerical collar, and suddenly I was confronted in my spirit by the Holy Spirit of God with the uncomfortable question, "What are you going to do with this man?" My first reaction was to respond, "I don't intend to do anything with him! And I am certainly not going to pick him up and give him a ride."

In true Pharisee fashion, I passed on by him and drove for several blocks before the painful question came back to me again, "What are you going to do with this man?" By then, I had finally realized that the Spirit of God was dealing with me about this matter.

For the next few hours, the Holy Spirit persistently convicted me of my strong prejudices toward other religions, and toward other parts of the Christian Church. This came as a surprise to me, but once again, my confident and boastful words from the past came back to haunt me: "Any man who wears his collar backwards obviously does not know what direction he is going!" Once again, I could hear the congregation's loud calls of approval in response to my blatant statement of religious prejudice. That was when I realized I had been making a serious mistake. Now I would have to deal with more than just racial prejudice—God wanted me to confront religious prejudice in my own heart and in the hearts of others as well.

I must say that at the time I made those prejudiced remarks, I was totally unaware that my statements were prejudicial. Nor was it in my heart to have negative feelings toward other church groups. After all, I was "born" a Pentecostal boy, went to a Baptist college, and graduated from a Methodist seminary! I even took some classes at a Presbyterian seminary. How could I have prejudice in my heart against anyone of another denomination or belief? No matter how I justified or rationalized the issue, it kept surfacing in my mind over and over again. The Spirit's desire was clear: I would have to deal with this issue if I wanted to go on in the Kingdom of God.

To my complete surprise, I felt impressed of the Holy Spirit that I should put on a clerical collar as a visible statement of my victory over prejudice. I sensed that it would also serve as a bridge between the liturgical churches and my own denomination or family of like faith. I thought to myself, *How ridiculous this is going to be for me—a Pentecostal preacher—to wear a clerical collar!* I had never heard of such a thing in my entire life. I pondered it for several days, and committed it to prayer.

I had already worn a clerical collar on a few occasions during the early Civil Rights clashes, and also to gain entrance to downtown hospitals. In those days, the clergy were still greatly respected in nearly every class of society, so the clerical collar offered some measure of protection from many of the rioters in the streets of Atlanta. As I recall, I bought my first "collar" during the early Civil Rights era from the Lutheran store, and none of us knew how to put the thing on.

Wearing a collar in a crisis situation was one thing, but wearing a collar as a regular lifestyle was unheard of for any "respectable" Pentecostal preacher. Questions kept echoing in my mind: *How could this be God? I would be wearing a clerical collar not only with the eyes of my own local church upon me, but also in the full view of my fellow brethren in Charismatic and Pentecostal circles! What would they think?*

I remember the first Sunday morning that I walked to the pulpit wearing my clerical collar. The people in the congregation looked at me in amazement, but no one seemed to have the courage to ask me what I was doing with my collar on "backwards." (At least no one asked me if I knew where I was going.) When I stepped behind the pulpit, I openly confessed the religious prejudices I had toward other churches.

I had been taught as a boy that the Roman Catholic Church was the "harlot church" of Revelation! This was so deeply drilled into my thinking that I didn't see any reason for me to address this matter. It became very confusing, however, when I heard that several million Roman Catholics had received the baptism of the Holy Spirit. I began to wonder why God would "allow" these people to receive the baptism of the Holy Spirit if, in fact, they belonged to the "harlot church."

I got through the service all right with little or no negative responses to my clerical collar. I encouraged the pastors on our presbytery to wear a collar as well, at least for a time, to symbolize our overcoming any prejudice in religion whatsoever. I thought to myself, *This is a much better way to correct my wrongs than the course God required of the Old Testament prophet,*

Isaiah! He had to walk down the streets of Egypt and Ethiopia without any clothes on for three whole years![1]

The congregation seemed to be very content and happy with the fact that we were wearing clerical collars. It helped their children quickly identify their pastors, which was important since we had grown to a rather large congregation. The collars also opened many new doors of ministry to our pastors. No longer did we have to stand in line to gain entrance to hospitals—we were recognized as clergy and admitted on sight. We soon found that when any one of our ministers encountered an emergency along a highway or in a public place, he was immediately accepted as a clergyman and his assistance was readily received.

Despite the many positive benefits of wearing the clerical collar, I still felt very strange when I went among my brethren, particularly my Charismatic and Pentecostal brethren. I knew that some of them privately suspected that my collar was some kind of a statement of pride, or that I had lost my Pentecostal fervor. The fact was neither of these suspicions was true. The collar was more a public sign of correction and confession before others than a statement of spiritual pride or ministerial achievement.

As you may know, it is now quite common to see Pentecostal preachers of all persuasions wearing clerical collars. This publicly signifies a new cooperation between the liturgical church and the Charismatic church, and it also gives the ministers of God immediate identification in public places.

Police officers wear certain types of uniforms, as do many other professional and official public servants. Why shouldn't a preacher of the gospel be identified by his clothing? After all, this was the pattern of the Old Testament. Priests were certainly known by their clothing.

As time went by, I became even more comfortable with the idea that this "collar thing" was a move of God to break down barriers between religious groups. Some of the greatest prejudice in Pentecostal circles was against the Roman Catholic Church and the Episcopal Church. Although I do not and probably never will agree with portions of the doctrines embraced by these churches, I still felt God wanted us to make a positive statement about our unity around the cross of Christ. That is why we stayed with it all these years.

---

1. See Isaiah 20:2-3.

There were certain ministers and ministries that adopted the convention of wearing clerical collars in a big way in the early days—but as soon as the newness and novelty wore off, they quit because they had no conviction supporting their actions. In contrast, our conviction at the Cathedral of the Holy Spirit is just as strong today as it was then because God burned the issue of religious prejudice into my heart. (By the way, we don't wear a Catholic collar; we wear Episcopal collars that we purchase at a Lutheran bookstore, if that makes any difference.)

In my travels around the world, I have often been approached by hurting people in airports and public terminals asking for spiritual guidance. On many occasions, I have come upon accidents where there was an immediate need for prayer. From the first day I donned a "collar" to this one, I have always been well received in these situations because the clerical collar I was wearing plainly set me apart as a representative of the Church. I, in no way, suggest that others wear the collar. I am only saying that to us, the clerical collar has become a symbol of togetherness with the Body of Christ and has served somehow as a bridge between the liturgical church and the Pentecostal and Charismatic brethren.

At this writing, the ministers at Chapel Hill Harvester Church have been wearing clerical collars for many years, although it is not a mandatory requirement. It has become a statement of our commitment to walk in harmony with the Christian Church at large.

I came to a better appreciation of this when I was chosen as one of nine theologians from the Pentecostal family of churches to dialogue with leading Roman Catholic brethren several years ago. Much of our dialogue was centered around areas where we realized there would never be agreement, yet we did feel an agreement in the Spirit!

We discussed everything from the infallibility of the Pope to infant baptism, but our dialogue was done in such a proper and orderly manner, and in such a good spirit, that God really spoke to all of us. We learned, above everything else, that there was one Lord and one Church. We realized that we had to allow those walls to fall down if, in fact, we were committed to let the world know that Jesus Christ is the Lord.

At the conclusion of our Pentecostal and Catholic dialogue, we defied tradition and shared the table of the Lord. It was done in such a way that we all realized the presence of Christ was among us. To my amazement, many of the Roman Catholic theologians were Spirit-filled, and they clearly praised God in a spiritual language without inhibition. I came to appreciate the fact that many of these dedicated men of God were certainly "called" and mightily used of God in our day.

Throughout our discussions in the Catholic monastery where the meetings were conducted, we were all well aware of the different views we held concerning the Eucharist, or the Lord's Table. After we had discussed our different views of the "elements" (the wine and bread), the Catholic priests and theologians realized that we clearly understood that if we shared the Lord's Table with them and drank from the cup of wine, that we were not drinking to the Pope. Once we cleared that away, we had a basis for joint communion in Christ.

The intimate communion service we shared together was a beautiful experience in which the anointing of the Holy Spirit was clearly present. I later went to see Father Scanlan, a Roman Catholic priest and scholar who was the head of a school at Steubenville, Ohio. As we talked about the divisions between the Roman Catholic Church and the Protestant churches, particularly the Pentecostal circles, we began to talk about the issue of communion.

This godly and very charismatic priest literally broke into tears as he said to me, "You don't know how it grieves me to know that we can't even come together over the body of Christ. Something has got to be resolved somewhere down the line." I couldn't agree with him more—it is time for the Body of Christ to gather together again as a family around the cross, and around the feet of Him who has purchased us out of every tribe and nation.

We cannot deal with racial prejudice if we continue to ignore prejudice among church leaders and religious groups. What must the unsaved world think when it sees the battles waged between "conservative" and "liberal" Christians, with brutal and unloving accusations flying in both directions? No wonder the world stands back and asks the question, "So these people serve a 'good' God?"

The widespread competition between churches and religious communities sends a clear signal to the world that something is seriously wrong in the Body of Christ. Ask yourself, "Are there many bodies of Christ? Or is there one body of Christ with many members?"[2] The time has come for us to deal with these issues if we intend to impact the world as we should. We can no longer afford to have our own pet ideas. It is time for us to seek the face of God so we can present a truly united front to oppose and defeat the forces that oppose the Kingdom of God.

We can no longer afford the luxury of our own opinions and ideas—we must find and fully yield to the mind of God. According to the Book of Romans, only the Holy Spirit knows the true mind of the Father.[3] We must give ourselves to the guidance of the Holy Spirit as never before so we can send a clear message to our dying and hurting world.

I can remember the first time I walked into a group of Pentecostal and Charismatic preachers while wearing a clerical collar. I saw every eye turn to examine me as if I were some sort of alien from another planet. No one actually confronted me or said anything negative, but it was obvious that there were many questions in the minds of the brethren.

Although I can certainly understand this, I still must reply that it is time for the Body of Christ to go beyond the mere milk of the Word—we must stop judging people according to what they wear. Shallow outward standards of righteousness passed away the day Jesus was nailed to the tree on Golgotha. Please hear me when I say this: "Far too many times, we are so clothes-conscious that we lose sight of our calling." The cost of a tie today is almost unbelievable, yet many times we look at a man's apparel and costly array as if it were some heavenly symbol of success in the ministry. It seems to me that we lost something along the way that could be quickly regained—if we will only realize that we do not represent ourselves, but the Church of the Lord Jesus Christ.

We need to lay down our swords of criticism, ridicule, and disdain for one another so we can begin to understand and appreciate each other. Controversy arose in recent years over the "outbreak of laughter" in the worship services of certain Charismatic fellowships, and some of the worshipers appeared to be "barking" or making other strange sounds during the ministry. Rather than arbitrarily judging (and dismissing) these matters, perhaps

---

2.   1 Corinthians 12:12-14.
3.   Romans 8:26-27.

we should stop and ask ourselves, "What is God doing?" Maybe this is a sign that points to something else that is about to take place. Or it could be that God is tearing down our inhibitions to open us up to a time of pure and wonderful praise.

Perhaps this is a modern day adaptation of a "mud in the eyes" healing, or "snake on a pole" symbol of a greater move yet to come. I understand what a fad can do. Fads come and go, even in Christian or religious circles. But it seems to me that there is no place for us to stand in criticism one against the other. Perhaps God has something in His mind that we have not yet clearly defined, but in no case can we afford to embrace or participate in religious prejudice.

No one is a greater admirer of Benny Hinn than I am. I appreciate his message, his ministry, and the healing that he has brought to thousands. Many question the methods by which people experience what some call "being slain in the Spirit." I have heard many criticisms of the methods employed in Brother Hinn's ministry; however, I urge believers to stop and perceive what God is doing. He is calling attention to the fact that He is a good God. I have also found that no one leads people into a greater sense of praise and adoration of God than Benny Hinn. No one who has the Spirit of God can deny that there is a tremendous presence of God in these meetings. The bottom line is that many people are being healed and saved through this ministry, and for this we give God the glory.

I remember the deluge of disapproval we received when we began to have choreographed dance in our church. We had letters and phone calls from all over the nation calling us everything but Christians. Now that several years and barriers have been spanned, it is quite common to see interpretive dance in Pentecostal and Charismatic churches around the world. We are entirely too quick to judge a matter before its time. Perhaps we should be more understanding toward others in terms of the types of worship offered to God in the Church today.

When we decided to allow our youth group to bring the rock sound into their youth services many years ago, we again received a flood of criticism from all around the country. Our critics loudly proclaimed that all rock music was "of the devil." However, many powerful young ministers came out of that movement. These young men and women are working in the Kingdom of God as full-time ministers of the gospel today because we dared to preach Christ through a new and totally unfamiliar medium.

We have now come to the place where "alternative music" is very popular among Christian young people around the world. We are again asking ourselves the question in our own church, "How far can we go in our own youth services to allow our young people to use the music that they are accustomed to today?" My overall feeling is that we should be very careful not to judge our young people too quickly. They may well be the vanguard of the army God is raising up to minister to this generation!

I am sure the Church of the Lord Jesus Christ in the twenty-first century will take on many new looks, sounds, and strategies that will be totally unfamiliar to us. The important thing to look for as time goes along, is for the Church to move toward true unity in Christ. We must come to fully understand that we are all walking under the same banner of love. The same blood of Jesus Christ that purges each one of us from our sins is one blood, and it is creating one Church united, not many churches divided.

The Acts of the Apostles clearly records how the Holy Spirit made every attempt possible to bring together the widely diverse believers in Jerusalem and abroad into one body. Some were from Jewish backgrounds, and others were Gentiles. Yet again and again, God spoke to His people about dwelling together in a spirit of unity. From the revolutionary vision of multiracial salvation Peter received on the housetop in Acts 11:5-10, to Paul's forays into Gentile areas of the world to preach the gospel in Ephesians 3:8, one common theme dominates the advancement of the Kingdom of God: the Body of the risen Christ should be one.

Just as racial prejudice can never be erased apart from a life-changing experience with God, so must we commit to real obedience to the Spirit of Christ to come into unity with the Body of Christ. Many express a deep-seated fear about any concept of there being "one church" in the world, because they confuse the Church of Jesus Christ with man-made ecumenical compromises devoid of the divine Savior and risen Lord, and with the "harlot church" of end-time eschatology.

However, whether we cry against it or support it, the fact is that there is only one Church of the Lord Jesus Christ. It may be divided into many groups, and it may be spread out around the world, but the fact remains that there is but one Body of Christ. If we are to be true disciples of the Lord Jesus Christ, then we must open ourselves by the Spirit to our brothers and sisters around the world.

The Church that Christ is building must declare without apology that it is only through the blood of Jesus Christ that we may be forgiven of our sins. Unity of the Spirit does not and never will entail compromise with religions that have discarded the chief cornerstone, Jesus Christ.

I believe that the greatest last day battles will be between those who follow the risen Christ, and those who discount the truth that Jesus Christ is the Messiah. Although this battle may be in the future, we must still live and preach by certain unchanging principles.

When the Body of Christ comes together, then we can do battle in the heavenlies to bring about the return of Christ, our Lord. We cannot do this as a Christian body when we are divided and fragmented. It is only when we can speak with authority as one voice that the world and opposing forces will hear and be influenced. The truth is that the world is still waiting to hear that common voice. It is up to us to lay down our petty differences and stand in agreement as one unified body. Only then will we be able to proclaim God's solutions for the future with the "voice of the Bride," and stand against the evils of the day.

Chapter 8

From Babel to Pentecost

Countless times over the years people have asked me, "How can a person bring about integration like you have at the Cathedral at Chapel Hill?" My answer is always the same: "There must first be an experience." Any minister's preaching must consistently reflect his deepest convictions across the years. People are very discerning, and they know when they are hearing a sermon designed to "satisfy the ear."

All great moves of God come from the preaching of truth. Every time the truth of God is violated (regardless of the reason), we just have to go around the mountain again. Many of us circle the mountain again and again while hoping to see the "manifestation and revelations" of God that we think will eventually bring to pass the coming of Jesus Christ.

Once I realized that the Bride of Christ is made up of every "race, tribe, and tongue" of mankind that ever lived on this planet, then I knew that God wants to have that depth and breadth of variety demonstrated in His Church today. I believe that there is absolutely no excuse for the division of the races in the house of God! I can almost hear the voices of many people protesting in their hearts, if not with their tongues: "But you don't understand—God has made us different, and we should respect that difference!"

I must answer with a warning: "Remember that our racial differences came about because of rebellion at the tower of Babel, according to Genesis 11:1-9." According to the Bible record, we are now in the process of restoring God's family into unity. Pentecost was certainly the reverse of what took place at Babel eons before.

According to the Book of Acts, when the believers went to the streets after being baptized in the Holy Spirit on Pentecost, the Jewish people who had gathered in Jerusalem from many nations "were confounded, because that every man heard them speak in his own language."[1] The "tongue-talkers" might not have known what language they were speaking, but to the ears of the hearers, it was a common language. God was correcting man's errors of the ancient past. I firmly believe every Spirit-filled believer today must be listening to hear what the Spirit is saying.

What is the Spirit saying to the Church today? The Spirit of God had a specific message for each of the seven churches in Asia Minor. In the same way, I believe the Spirit of God has a message for the Church today. I believe that message has to do with the maturing of the Body of Christ.[2]

I believe the hour has come for the Bride to mature and come to full age, so the Father can send His Son back to complete the marriage for which we have all been praying. I do not believe this can take place as long as there is any evidence of racial prejudice in the Body of Christ. The hour has come for us to single-heartedly seek God with such fervor that all the walls of partition will be broken down, and there will no longer be separation in the family of God.

When Jesus Christ died on the cross, the Word of God tells us the veil was "rent in twain from the top to the bottom."[3] I believe it was the hands of God that gripped the veil from the very top, and ripped it from top to bottom—not from bottom to top. That was God's dramatic way of saying that all that separates God and man, and man from man, must now be taken down.

When Jesus was asked, "What are the most important commandments?" He quickly replied, "First of all, love God with all your heart, and love your neighbor as yourself."[4] When someone asked Him on another occasion, "Who is my neighbor?" Jesus gave him the dramatic answer, "Your neighbor is the one who is in need."[5] If these Bible accounts are true, then

1.   Acts 2:6.
2.   Revelation 19:7; 21:2.
3.   Matthew 27:51.
4.   Matthew 22:36-40, my paraphrase.
5.   From Luke 10:29-37.

the veil was torn so there would not be any separation between God and man or between man and man.

The hour is growing late. We are approaching the twenty-first century, and God is waiting for a people whom He can trust with truth.[6] He is looking for people who have been purged of prejudice and have uprooted bitterness.[7] It must be a people who can be referred to as being absolutely "pure in heart."[8]

Some leaders in the Body of Christ have been called out to be "special witnesses" in critical areas of need. For example, I believe some people have been called out to remind us that God has power to deliver and to heal.[9] Others were born to remind us of the vital need to diligently study and apply God's Word in our lives. Still others have been called of God to exhort us to "train up our children in the fear of the Lord" in private Christ-centered schools. There are even leaders in the Church who have been called forth in our day as living "signs" pointing toward certain future occurrences of great importance to the Body of Christ. Without exception, all of these have been called to speak God's heart, not only to the Church, but to the world.

I firmly believe that God has called me to be a "special witness" to the utter importance of true unity in the Body of Christ. I do not believe you can separate the power of the Holy Ghost, the gospel of the Kingdom, and the message of unity. These three must run side by side. The gospel of the "rule of Christ" is essential because it brings us into obedience unto one Lord. The message of unity is at the very core of God's heart, and we hear it played out in chapter 17 of John by Jesus Christ Himself.

I have related at other times and in other writings that I have been very much aware of the ministry of the late David DuPlessis. Only eternity will reveal the role this man played in bringing unity to the Body of Christ. He boldly defied the religious taboos of his day to break down many of the walls between the Roman Catholic Church and the Protestant churches (including Pentecostals) during the Charismatic Renewal among Catholic

6.   John 16:12-13.
7.   Hebrews 12:14-15.
8.   Matthew 5:8.
9.   2 Peter 1:12.

priests and nuns. He was far ahead of his time when he exhorted us to focus on the essential things God wants us to preach, teach, and live instead of allowing ourselves to be divided by less important or even frivolous issues.

I remember the day I was called into a hotel room by David DuPlessis, along with my friend, Bishop John Meares. Brother DuPlessis told us, "God has spoken to me to lay my hands upon both of you so that you might pick up the mantle that I will soon be laying down." I never will forget those aged hands that were laid upon my head as he prayed, "Let this voice continue through this man's preaching." I can truly say that Brother DuPlessis' prayer was both a confirmation and yet another spiritual deposit spurring me on in my belief and conviction that the Body of Christ must be in unity.

Now I know why, as a Pentecostal-born boy, I was educated in a Baptist college, further trained in a Methodist seminary, and became deeply involved in many ecumenical movements. I believe God was preparing me to do exactly what I am doing in this book: declaring that the Body of Christ is one blood, and that we must lay aside our differences and everything that causes us to regard one another with suspicion. It is time to realize that we are brothers and sisters in Christ.

If you make an incision on the wrist of any human being on this planet, the blood that comes out will be red. It makes no difference what color the skin may be—the blood within looks alike! Even the most avowed racist in the world can be saved in a medical emergency through a transfusion of blood from a member of the race he hates the most! Why? Within the minor limitations of specific blood type compatibility, human blood is interchangeable. As the Scriptures declared long ago, we were created a people of one blood.

This seems to be something in the natural that is indicative of the spiritual. Did not the Word of the Lord say, "First the natural, then the spiritual"?[10] When the blood of Jesus Christ drained from His body on the cross, it was not only red blood, it was also totally pure blood, untainted by sin or rebellion! It is through His precious blood that we have now been bought with a price. His sacrifice allows us to enter into the family of God, making

---

10. 1 Corinthians 15:46.

us of one blood. Now if this is true (and it is), how can we dare to accuse or to condemn one another? How can we justify separating ourselves from one another or trying to "prove our differences" or racial superiority over one another? God did away with all that. Now we are to devote our energies instead to proving the fact that we are literally one in the Body of Christ! It is this miracle above all others that will mark us as the disciples of Christ.[11]

I have often said that I do not know what Heaven will really be like. It is safe to say that I probably know the Scriptures as well as most, but I now know that no mortal can describe what this heavenly experience will be like in eternity. I often say, "Hell is an extension of an evil life that continues in the same direction eternally." Perhaps those born again of the Spirit will find that Heaven is just an extension of what we are becoming here and now! If this is true, then Heaven certainly will be a place where only those who have settled their prejudices can live together in peace.

How can we even imagine living together in peace in Heaven when we cannot do so on earth? Perhaps we should start praying that things would "be done in earth, as [they are] in heaven."[12] I think all of us would agree that there are no prejudices in Heaven. My question is why does our agreement stop there? Groceries won't do anyone any good unless they are brought home and served at the table.

Whatever else Heaven may be, I have often wondered if I will see Sammy again in the heavenly realm. If so, I would like to look at him and say in all truth, "Sammy, I made a promise to you in the cotton patches of South Georgia while we stood upon planet Earth. In the years that have passed, I have been faithful to that vow, my friend."

That will be a glorious time when we live together in the family of God eternally. I am sure there will be activities in Heaven as well as on this purged and renewed earth. Whatever they are like, the one thing I know is that Heaven will be a place of total peace and harmony between all people. As we enter the twenty-first century, we need to know that it will be this kind of thinking and this kind of Church that will lay aside all the difficulties and differences we have experienced across the years. It is time for the

11. John 13:35.
12. Matthew 6:10.

ax to be laid to the root of prejudice and hatred. It is time to live in covenant relationship with unity in the Body of Christ.

I can hear my baby sister, Joan, who has already gone to Heaven, singing the song of years past that says, "Saved, by the blood of the Crucified One." I know that she is experiencing what we are now preaching. She is dwelling with a celestial family that has gathered together in the very presence of God. The apostle Paul made it abundantly clear when he wrote, "To be absent from the body, [is] to be present with the Lord."[13]

Whatever else Heaven is like, we know from God's Word that it will be a place where those who are gathered around the Father Himself, saints drawn out of every nation and every tongue, will be able to praise Him with one voice and with one spirit.

Why are we waiting to be translated, resurrected, or raptured sometime in the indiscernible future for such fellowship and communion with God and man? Why shouldn't we begin practicing now for what Heaven will be like then? If we would put this heavenly vision in our minds, we would see through eyes that have been sanctified and with hearts that have been set apart to do God's will. The hour is growing late, but it is not too late! Let us move toward that glorious prize that has been set aside for us. We would then fellowship with one another right now as God has planned from the beginning.

---

13.   2 Corinthians 5:8.

Our Field Is the World

(Anthony Lockett, Cathedral Praise Publ. ©1995. Used with permission.)

In the lands far away
People hunger for days
Of tranquillity for the human race
From the ocean's blue waves
To the mountains and caves
They hope and pray for equality.

CHORUS:
Our field is the world
Every heart is a pearl
All people of color
Are our brothers and sisters.

(Swahili)
Uwanja yetu ni dunia
Kila moyo no dhahabu
Watu wa kila kabila
Wana undugu nasi

Although we may not agree
In all things verbally
We're on the same team of fulfilling dreams
We must shine our light
In the darkness of the night
Leading the way to a resting place

BRIDGE:
We were made to fly high like an eagle
Gliding on the airwaves, speaking to all people

(Spanish)
Nuestro campo es almundo

(Japanese)
Karitori no ba wa Sekai
Subete no Kokoro Shinju

Donna iro no hada demo
Bokumno Kyodai shimai

CHORUS

Chapter 9

Born to Be a Racist

I wrote this book as more of a testimony than an historical account of the racial problem. Yet as I recalled all the challenges and events I've seen over the years, I have asked myself again and again, "Lord, why am I so strong on the subject of racial harmony?"

That leads naturally to the larger question, "What makes any man or woman what or who they are?" I have asked the question many times, "Why me, Lord?" After all, I had every reason in the world to grow up as a very prejudiced white man: I was born in the deep South; I was converted in a church that had very strong racial segregation guidelines that separated the races; I grew up in a godly family that nevertheless very strongly opposed any sort of interracial marriage or even interracial activities. Given the generally segregationist circumstances of my birth and upbringing, what caused me to become so absolutely convinced that I was called of God to bring harmony between the races?

As I thought of the many experiences I have related to you, I realized most of them had a lasting effect upon my life. Yet none of them was strong enough to deeply propel me into the struggle to bring about peace between the races.

I recall the many times I became embroiled in heated discussions about the racial problems of the day. I usually stood alone in those arguments because I was expressing my deepest convictions, not merely ideas or contrary counterpoints. I have wondered why God chose me to take a stand for equality that has been consistent in my ministry for 52 years. The road hasn't been easy, but the rewards have been immeasurably rich.

What causes anyone to be who he is, or to follow convictions despite danger or possible death? What stirred and inspired Martin Luther King, Jr., to become the nation's greatest outspoken voice against racial prejudice is those dark days early in the Civil Rights Movement? Was it because he was born to godly parents? Was it because he was educated in institutions that gave him intellectual foundations for his heartfelt convictions? I don't think so.

I believe that Martin Luther King, Jr., had a visitation from God. That single encounter with the Creator gave him a direction and destiny for his life from which he never varied—even in the face of possible death or injury. He was a preacher of preachers. You can hear it in the tone of his voice—he was simply speaking what was in his heart.

What transformed Joseph from a baby brother into the deliverer of the starving Hebrew nation? What happened in the life of Peter to help him overcome his inbred and culturally reinforced racial hatred to the point that he willingly took the gospel to the Gentiles? We may not be able to come up with a single answer.

What caused Mother Teresa to devote her entire life to reaching out to the dying and the hungry members of a non-Christian nation? Why has she spent her life trying to help such a mass of hurting people? I do not believe that anyone can say exactly what happened to Mother Teresa, unless he has heard her share something out of her own heart.

I have devoted my life to preaching and teaching a gospel of reconciliation between the races, declaring that we are "one blood, under God." It was the faithfulness I learned to exhibit in these areas that triggered another experience with God one Saturday night that was to totally change my life.

I was taught as a young preacher that "the Kingdom of God" was not something to be addressed presently. That term was exclusively reserved for the "thousand-year reign" that would take place after the tribulation, when Jesus Christ would return to rule and reign for a millennium. Since I had been taught this all my life, I simply put it out of my mind. I did not realize that the Kingdom of God was timeless and eternally existent. In fact, there has never been a time when God's Kingdom was not active. I wasn't consciously seeking to learn anything about what may be called a "gospel of the Kingdom of God."

I went to bed one Saturday night and had a vision in which the Spirit of God took me through the Book of Revelation. He showed me a totally new insight that I had never learned through my own studies. I quickly realized that it was the story of a victorious Christ who was to become King of kings and Lord of lords.[1]

I saw many glimpses of the particular battles that would eventually bring together a nation of believers under the banner of His Kingship. I also saw the throne of God surrounded by a circular rainbow, and the color of emerald green stood out from all the rest.[2] More than anything else, I was aware of the "eternal nowness" of God.[3]

I heard the groanings of the earth, and I remember asking, "What are the groanings that I hear?" Then this Voice answered, "The groanings upon the earth are from those waiting for the demonstration of the Kingdom of God." Some would refer to this as the manifestation of the sons of God.[4] Since this phrase has been prostituted in certain theories and doctrines, I prefer to avoid using it in this manner.

The groanings were because there was such strife, hatred, bitterness, and prejudice on the face of the earth, and the whole world was groaning to see a demonstration of a loving community.

When I woke up, my pillow was wet with tears. The next morning was Sunday, and when I went to the pulpit to tell my congregation about the vision, my voice broke as I described my experience with God.

I didn't realize it at the time, but I now believe that God could trust me with revelation of the Kingdom of God because I had been faithful in the spiritual battle against racial prejudice. This gave me a new motivation to deal even more radically with the issues tied to the race problem.

In the months that followed, I searched and prayed repeatedly that God would unfold the last book of the Bible to me, the Revelation of Jesus Christ.[5] Although I had been a student of God's Word all my life, the Bible suddenly seemed like a new book to me! Pieces of the eschatology and

---

1. Revelation 6:16-17; 19:16.
2. Revelation 4:3.
3. Revelation 1:8.
4. Romans 8:19-23.
5. Ephesians 1:17.

theology puzzle began to fit together. One teaching I did on "Body Life" during that period launched ministries of restoration and deliverance from the bondage of satan in people's lives.

God directed me to teach "Spiritual Authority" next. For months, I preached sermons on the Kingdom of God: the Kingdom mind, Kingdom giving, Kingdom lifestyles, and the "pearl of great price" as a symbol of the Kingdom of God on earth.[6]

I literally ate, drank, slept, talked, and preached the Kingdom night and day. I was consumed with the nowness of God, and the awesome reality of God in the flesh in His Church.[7] I pressed believers everywhere to live out responsible Christianity as bold sons and daughters of the King. My proclamation of the Kingdom of God soon ignited the wrath of the opposing kingdom.[8] Satan attacked the leadership of the church and successfully stirred up discord, misunderstandings, and rebellion among the brethren.

Prophetic exhortation from elders warned me repeatedly, "Do not look at the faces of the people as you preach," but even so I could often feel hostility bounce back in response to my words of exhortation and instruction. It was the same feeling I had experienced in those early days of my ministry when I first preached against racial prejudice.

Some of the leaders of the church, including some beloved family members, warned me not to speak the things God Himself had commanded me to say. Many fell away from the uncompromised calling of our church, and I am referring to very sincere people who loved God. I wept over them in intercession, but I had put my hand to the plow. I could not look back.

It was such a mystery to me why people weren't as thrilled about this vision of the Kingdom of God as I was, no matter how hard I tried to explain it to them. Things took a turn for the worse when the messages were aired on television, because many pastors across the country became upset.

Carl Barth once said, "Truth is on the razor edge of heresy." I began to feel like I was being cut by that "razor of truth" nearly every day. When I was a young man, God asked me to reveal the desire of my heart and He

---

6.   Matthew 13:45-46.
7.   Galatians 4:19; Colossians 1:27.
8.   Matthew 24:7; Revelation 12:12.

would grant it. I said, "Lord, I want the gift of love. I want to love Your people." I was very comfortable being a pastor, and our church members, pastoral staff, and television viewers were comfortable with my role as a pastor too.

However, once I started preaching about the spiritual authority of Christ the King, and the reign of Christ in every area of our lives, I quickly became very unpopular. I suppose no one wanted to hear this prophetic message.

I was deeply hurt by this unexpected rejection because God had given me the gift of love, and I desperately wanted to please everyone. Then I met Pastor John Garlington from Portland, Oregon. This man heard the wind of the Spirit. He spoke eloquently, powerfully, and confidently, because he served the Lord as a prophetic mouthpiece to His Church.

I first met John when he attended the first Pastor's Conference our church hosted in Atlanta in the fall of 1982. In October of 1984, our paths crossed again. This time we met at a conference held at Evangel Temple in Washington, D.C. Bishop John Meares had invited both John Garlington and myself to share in that conference. Brother Garlington was standing at the podium delivering a powerful address when he suddenly turned to me and began to prophesy these words directly to me:

"It's kind of funny…sometimes God shows me comical pictures. I saw this little scenario in the comic strip 'Peanuts.' Each year when the football season begins, the little girl holds the football, and the little boy runs to kick it. Each time he gets there, she moves it and he falls—then he comes back next year.

"Something has happened over the years as you have reached out and touched people; and [there are] two things I have sensed being around you (and I'm kind of glad I won't be around you for awhile):

"There is an intense burden in your spirit to see the birth of the Kingdom of God. That intensity bothered me at first. I didn't know what was going on. All of a sudden, I became aware that I was just feeling that intensity in your spirit. And there is such an intensity in your spirit about seeing the Kingdom of God birthed, seeing a visible demonstration of it, that people who get around you don't really understand. They feel that your orientation is on the Kingdom and not the King. But they don't understand that God has uniquely raised you up as a part of the birthing process in the earth. You are literally one of those who is feeling a sense of violence and pressure in your spirit to birth the Kingdom of God.

"You reach out to touch. Over and over again, you've touched people who then move the football. But God has called you not only to see the victories and the joys of the Kingdom, but you're one that God is using to fill up the sufferings. That is unusual because we hear so much today about the message of prosperity and the message of victory, but Paul said that we are also called to 'fill up the sufferings of Jesus Christ.'

"I see inside your body such wounds and bruises until when the opportunity comes to reach out and heal again, sometimes you are concerned, because you are aware of the bruises that come. Sometimes, even while you are reaching out, there is a sense in your spirit that the bruise will come again. I don't understand that. I wish I could give you a word of relief, but it's the glory and the suffering that God has caused you to feel in your spirit.

"God wants you to know that you are going to see fantastic things happen in southeastern America. God has raised you up, man of God, as a beacon in that place.

"You've been 'a sign spoken against,' but I want you to know that God is raising you up as a spiritual Joseph, because as famine begins to fill the spiritual land, men are going to come to you and say, 'We don't understand it; we were offended by what you did.' But you are going to say like Joseph, 'The things you meant for evil, God meant for good.' It will not be many days until those who have caused the pain and bruises are going to come back again and say, 'We were wrong; God has dealt with us in the night hours. There was an anointing on our ministry that is gone.' They are going to come back for healing at your hands.

"I just know that until you have fulfilled what God is doing in you, you are always going to feel stretched beyond measure. There is such a sense in my own spirit of what you feel, of that urgency of the Kingdom in your heart, that thing in you that just cries out to God to see a birthing go on. It's such an intense thing that you find yourself eating and sleeping the Kingdom of God. You are a man whom God has consumed with that desire. The Kingdom of Heaven does suffer violence, and that violence is going on in your spirit. But you are going to see release after release.

"Brother, God is going to *unbuckle the Bible belt. He is going to knock down tradition.* He is going to move in such a tremendous way. Even as you've said to people that thing that God is going to do, He is going to do it! There is going to come a revival in southeastern America that is going to shake the nations. It will be spoken of around the world, and God is going to make your place one of the focuses. God is going to make your place one of the pivotal points. God is going to make your place on the cutting edge of what He is doing in America.

"*And in the very place where sin, segregation, and discrimination have been so difficult, your place will become a sign to the nations of what happens when men move in the dimension of God's Kingdom.* And they will come from near and far to hear it. You will be able to say to them, 'It's a thing that is birthed in the Spirit. The Kingdom of God does not come by observation; it comes by revelation.'

"You have said, 'Hear me with your spirit,' and there is such a cry in you to have people hear with their spirits, and you wonder sometimes, 'Are they hearing?' There are people sprinkled around the nation who are beginning to hear with the ear of the Spirit and see with the eye of the Spirit, and God is using you as a provoker. Keep on provoking! The release is going to come.

"*It would seem, in ways that you cannot imagine, that part of the vision that God gave for the Atlanta area died, but it has not died.* It is going to be resurrected, and you are going to see double fruitfulness in the context of what you wanted to see in that city.

"I see you, Bishop, as a man like Jesus who has literally cried, and God is going to take those tears (He has kept them in a bottle), and you are going to come back, bringing in the sheaves with you. As much as you have known the pressures and burdens, you are going to know the joy of the Holy Spirit and the joy of harvest. Hallelujah!"

I was absolutely overcome when John Garlington ended his prophecy to me. I was to be a provoker. God help me! People hated me enough as it was. But I was so grateful for God taking the time to speak to me...to personally reassure me that I was on course...to promise that better days were coming...to let me know that my struggles of the past to bring equality to all men, regardless of the color of their skin, were not in vain.

Chapter 10

We Need a Blood Check

Why do we still see so much racial prejudice in the United States after all these years? Doesn't the U.S. Constitution and the First Amendment provide equality and freedom for all races alike? Isn't it true that the courts have upheld racial integration in schools, in businesses, and in all the other areas under government control? Haven't major church leaders met recently to discuss racial reconciliation?

Yes, all these things are true, but in spite of the progress we've seen in many areas, prejudice is alive and well. In fact, it may even be on the rise! At the time of this writing, the nation's daily newspapers and newsmagazines seem to be dominated by stories about an epidemic of racism in the military. One story told of two young white soldiers who had been accused of killing black people "simply because they did not like them."

Anyone who has served in the military recently will quickly confirm that racism is still an obvious problem in the ranks of our military organizations. Public schools that were integrated and making progress at one time have now become segregated again for the most part. Teachers and administrators in the schools that have remained integrated must maintain a constant watch to prevent violent battles between the races. The growing incidents involving guns in schools point to growing gang problems and increased violence. Many of these gangs are formed along racial lines for the protection of individuals in those gangs.

Can anyone deny that our churches are as segregated today as they were many years ago? Yes, there are some integrated churches in many of our major metro areas, but they are "few and far between." Although great black ministers are often invited to speak to mixed audiences, and certain white preachers sometimes speak to primarily black audiences on occasion, it is still true that segregation still has a firm grip on the religious world. The growing prominence of Louis Farrakhan and his racist gospel of the so-called Nation of Islam is but another clear sign that organized racism is on the rise in our nation.

The steady stream of news reports about people who are carrying Nazi flags or swastikas are constant reminders that there are still segments of our population who are still very much opposed to the presence of the black race. It is also not uncommon to hear resurrected terms like "black power" or other phrases dealing with the superiority or empowerment of black men. We are also hearing of more and more new beauty pageants and other competitive events organized solely along racial lines. All these things tell us that the battle is not over. Racial prejudice may be taking on a different form, but it is still a very dangerous and volatile element in our society.

I believe the reason we see prejudice and racism rising up again today is because the ax has not been laid to the root. We have dealt with surface issues and tried to deal with symptoms while doing little to really get to the heart of the matter. The heart of the matter is, in fact, the heart. "As a man thinketh in his heart, so his actions will be determined."[1]

It usually takes a true experience with God to shake us or our church out of our rigid thought patterns to see things from God's perspective. For the apostle Peter, who was steeped in his Hebrew concept, it took a dramatic vision to help him see that the redemption won at Calvary was for Gentiles as well as Jews. Even then, when he got to the house of Cornelius, he was heard to say, "I perceive that God is no respecter of persons."[2] He was saying, in essence, "I still may harbor prejudiced feelings toward non-Jewish races, but I see that God has moved beyond these fences and His work is more far-reaching than I had ever thought possible!"

As with so many of us today, the apostle Peter was still not totally cured of his racism. At a church gathering in a Gentile city later on, he withdrew from certain Gentile brethren when Jewish believers came to the

1.   Proverbs 23:7, my paraphrase.
2.   Acts 10:34.

meeting. The racial motivations were so obvious that the Bible says the apostle Paul withstood Peter to his face.[3] It seems apparent that the deeper purpose and plan of God's work among the nations of men hadn't penetrated Peter's heart. We are looking for "whatever it takes" to cure us of our prejudices from the inside out. We need to allow God's Spirit to move us beyond our own personal ideas and to change our hearts today.

It was no "accident" or coincidence that the 120 believers who came down from the upper room were ready to preach to people of all nations and tongues—they had been transformed and energized by an experience with God![4]

When our church first adopted the Bankhead Courts Public Housing Project, it was a real challenge to our white members. Since we had a relatively small number of black members at the time, the first volunteers for the work in the all-black Bankhead Courts project were white. Many of them provided tutoring assistance to students from the development, and others conducted literacy programs, scouting programs, recreational programs, and art classes.

As our church became more integrated, our black members also volunteered to go into this community where there were great needs. This only took place, however, because our people had a heartfelt conviction that this was a mission calling for their church. That is why they become involved.

At first, the work at Bankhead was thought of as a missionary endeavor. However, the beautiful thing was that after awhile our members, black and white, began to develop close relationships with the residents of Bankhead Courts. As a result, the people no longer thought of their respective races as being "different." We were ministering to people and their needs—with no thought about their race.

Our members often invited people from Bankhead into their homes for meals, and many times the children from the project came in to play with the children at our church. We also began to bring in busloads of boys and girls from the Bankhead area to our church to enjoy our swimming pool and play area, which includes a beach where volleyball can be played. After

3.   Galatians 2:11-12.
4.   Acts 2:1-10.

awhile, the racial and social lines drawn between these children just disappeared. Something had taken place in their hearts.

When it became apparent, recently, that a number of the young white teenagers in our "Teen to Teen" ministry were just as eager to minister among young unsaved black youths as were our black teenagers, I watched them very closely. I wanted to see if there were any adverse reactions to the differences in their races. I cannot give you a single account where this was true! As far as they were concerned, it was "teenagers ministering to teenagers," not "whites ministering to blacks."

We learned something that is critical to successful ministry in these areas: As long as we think of these areas of need as "sending people to the mission field," then we will never accomplish our goals. Success and genuine relationships will come only when we go to serve in humility, with the thought, "There, but for the grace of God, go I." Ministry in inner-city areas is complicated by the fact that many times, you must deal with poverty as well as racial problems.

Boatrock is another public housing development in the Atlanta area that houses hundreds of black families. Some time ago, we realized this community had a great need for a playground for its boys and girls, who had no place whatsoever where they could play outside. We helped to form a partnership between the Housing Authority of Fulton County, Georgia Tech, the Fulton County Parks and Recreation Department, and the Cathedral of the Holy Spirit. Our goal was simply to build a playground in this Boatrock housing development.

We decided who could provide what to make this mission come to pass. First, we had to get approval for the project from the Housing Authority, which controls any construction on the property. We also needed assistance from the Fulton County Parks and Recreation Department. They could oversee the project and help make the key construction decisions about the playground. But it was Georgia Tech that provided the architectural design that literally pictured for us what could be done on the muddy hillside we had to work with. The members of our church provided the primary manpower for the project.

We worked closely with parents from the Boatrock Projects, and with the Housing Authority and Georgia Tech to put together a beautiful playground. Important resources were also contributed by Delta Airlines and some local industries in the Atlanta area. It was an exciting day when we dedicated this facility and cut the ribbon. It was wonderful to see so many groups, most of which were white as far as the business community was concerned, join hands with the parents and residents of the Boatrock area, to help elevate the quality of life for some precious children. It was a glorious experience to dedicate that safe play area for the enjoyment of hundreds of children.

One of the most interesting things that happened during the project occurred when the Georgia Tech architectural students and staff took the children from Boatrock to existing playgrounds in the region. These adults asked the children to tell them what they would like to see in their playground. Of course, those children knew very well what they wanted. The most important thing about the trip was that it gave the children an identity and a feeling of being a part of what was taking place in their own community.

Change can take place wherever there is cooperation. When the church, the government, and the residents of an area put their hearts and minds together to accomplish specific goals, it can be done! We began to see something very unique take place. In the process of accomplishing a common goal, we witnessed a total breakdown of the obstacles between the races!

I believe there is a tremendous need today for what I call "the baptism of love." This experience will make us become color-blind, so we will see people according to their needs and potential, not their race or color. This baptism will cause us to fellowship in the things of the Spirit, because we are bought by the blood of Jesus Christ.

Several years ago, one lady in our church was dominated by extreme prejudice toward certain races and musical forms. One day she found she had cancer, and she began to seek God at a new level. In the midst of this, she had a glorious experience. She described it to the congregation as a "baptism of love." After this experience, she said she saw people in a totally different light. She went home to be with the Lord in great peace because she had been transformed by an experience with God, a beautiful baptism of love.

I do not believe that racial problems will ever be resolved apart from a true experience of the "baptism of love." It is God who empowers us to love people as they are instead of viewing them as "people who are different" from us. God is requiring us, as blood-washed members of His Church, to love one another enough to willingly give up our prejudices and personal feelings. That is the only way we can bring together the full family of God in all of its beauty under the Lord's banner of unconditional love.

It was this kind of experience on the road to Damascus that totally transformed Saul of Tarsus from a Christian-killing religious bigot into a soft-spoken loving apostle to all people.[5] This could never have taken place had he not gone through this glorious experience and emerged with the ability to see through new eyes and to feel with a new heart.

The apostle Paul later became God's greatest ambassador and evangelist to the entire non-Jewish world. He preached powerfully to both Jew and Gentile. At the end of his life, while awaiting a hearing before Caesar as a house prisoner in Rome, Paul devoted his energies to converting the Gentiles to the gospel of the Lord Jesus Christ.[6] How could this be? It happened because the apostle Paul had a glorious experience with God. Nearly every time he spoke to high potentates about his experience in his own defense, he told them about his life-changing encounter with Christ on the road to Damascus.

It seems to me that we need some "Damascus road experiences" today! We need some life-changing encounters to help us see people in a different light. We need to stop stereotyping people according to "politically correct" or "socially convenient" patterns, and begin to see them as God's chosen people instead. If we consider ourselves as part of God's people, then we have to accept the fact that we are part of a many-membered "family." In fact, God's Word calls us the "household of faith," and refers to us as a "body."[7]

If we are members one of another in this Body life experience, then we have no right to see or categorize ourselves according to racial groups. God puts it bluntly in His Word in many places and many ways. The bottom line is this: We are a family of one blood, bought by the same price, and living in a beautiful family relationship.

I love the old song that says, "What can wash away my sins? Nothing but the blood of Jesus." It is only through the blood of Jesus Christ that

5. Acts 26:9-20.
6. Acts 28:16,28-31.
7. Galatians 6:10; Colossians 3:15.

mankind can be cleansed of sin. We must remember Peter's revolutionary words on the housetop: "Whatever God has cleansed, do not call common or unclean."[8]

When the blood of Jesus Christ has been applied to a person, a family, or a race, something supernatural takes place that transcends and supercedes every personal idea and pet prejudice we might claim as our own. If we are foolish enough to cling to our soiled rags of prejudice and turn away from God's written salvation plan for man, then I believe we are trampling under foot the blood of Jesus Christ![9]

There is absolutely no biblical or logical justification for thinking that one race is superior to another! Any time and any place this devilish concept has taken root in a people or individual, it has always produced bitter division, strife, and even the callous killing of many innocent people.

This applies to people of every color, culture, and personal persuasion. In many communities where integrated congregations are found, certain members of black congregations will speak unkind words to black people who attend integrated churches. When a white man pastors many black members in an integrated congregation, it sometimes stirs up prejudice within people who attend totally black churches. But let me also hasten to tell you that is not always the case!

Thousands of our black members (and our white members as well) have had such an experience of the heart with God that they do not view me as a "white" pastor at all. They simply see me as a loving pastor. God has planted such a love between us that when I look at the members of the church, I know they would lay down their lives for me and for this vision.

One of the elderly ladies in our church, Leony Brown, is a real intercessor on my behalf and for my ministry. When I pass by her, I can literally feel the warmth of her love and the power of her prayers. Since I am in my sixty-ninth year, when I say she is an elderly warrior, you must know that she's been around for a long time. I feel such absolute support and love every time I pass her that she always encourages me. This is true of hundreds of others as well.

---

8. Acts 11:9, my paraphrase.
9. Hebrews 10:29.

When I go into any public place in the city of Atlanta where a number of black people are gathered, it is common for several people to walk up and thank me for the stand that I have taken on behalf of racial equality across the years. (Please understand that I have never felt that I needed any recognition for the stand I have taken—it is simply the stand that every Christian should take.) If Jesus declared, "Whosoever will...," then who am I to leave anyone out?[10]

It is time for the Church to be an example to the world in every matter of righteousness and ethical conduct. The world is anxiously waiting for leaders in the Church to speak out, and for us to demonstrate the kind of racial harmony and loving community life that will eventually bring peace in our nation.

As I have talked with several of the interracial couples in our church, I've learned that they still feel unaccepted, as if people are staring at them when they are in public. Prejudice is something that is rooted so deeply within us that we are usually not even aware that we think that way. As I watched a tennis match between a white girl and a black girl a few months ago, I noticed that my friend who was watching the match with me kept pulling for the white girl. Curious, I finally asked, "Why are you pulling for her?" Before he realized it, he said, "Because she is white."

It seems to me that we must deal with some of the hidden prejudices that have never been brought to light. That is why I say "the ax has not been laid to the root." We must test ourselves to be sure there is absolutely nothing within us that would hinder God's intention of having one family here on planet Earth. The household of faith is composed of people from every nation and tongue. Are we going toward the goal of living in true unity as a people of one blood, or have we started regressing to mindless divisions rooted in ancient prejudices again?

We need to call for a revival of heart. When a human heart is really changed, then human thinking patterns will change.[11] It is only this kind of life-changing encounter with God that will bring about the harmony He desires between the races.

10. Mark 8:34.
11. Mark 7:21.

Chapter 11

The Church of the Twenty-first Century

There is something very special about the ending of a millennium and the beginning of a new one. The year 2000 holds many anticipations and even mysteries. As we look forward to moving into a new dimension, we must seriously look at the role the Church will play.

We need some new definitions. It is difficult to explain to someone who has very little knowledge of the Church, why it is so varied and different. It is especially difficult to explain why it is so divided. The truth is that it is not only divided organizationally, but also in its beliefs and practices.

Before we can talk about one Church under one Lord with one baptism, paid for by the blood of Jesus Christ, we must begin to seriously contend with some of these questions. I believe there are a number of things that must take place if the Church is to be successful in the beginning of the new century.

1. The Church of the twenty-first century should have a thrust toward the central theme of the Bible.

If the central theme of God's Word is that "God so loved the world, that He gave His only begotten Son,"[1] then that must be the central message of the Church in the twenty-first century. We must discard any extra-biblical idea

---

1. John 3:16.

---

that the God of the universe is more kindly disposed toward one group than another.[2]

We must point out again and again, in various ways, that God loves the whole world, and that means all the people in the world—equally. As long as we make God in "our image" as a "God of preference," then we are automatically destroying the true image of God as the Maker and Creator of all the nations of the earth.

Although there are godless political systems in the world that stand against God and must be judged, we must never forget that God loves the people of the earth, as well as the earth itself. We need to clearly define and differentiate between the earth and the systems that run the world.[3] Over and over again, we must remind ourselves that the central theme of God's Word, and the theme of His heart, is that He loves every creature on this planet.

Another central theme of the Word of God is the dream of God, revealed by Jesus in the Gospel of John. Jesus was deeply concerned about unity. We cannot get away from the fact that in His compassionate "high priestly prayer" in the garden, Jesus prayed:

Neither pray I for these alone, but for them also which shall believe on Me through their word; that they all may be one; as Thou, Father, art in Me, and I in Thee, that they also may be one in Us: that the world may believe that Thou hast sent Me (John 17:20-21).

This certainly includes harmony among the various branches of the Body of Christ and among all the races of people gathered together in His name.

If the cry of Jesus Christ was that we may be one, then the church that is successful in the twenty-first century will be the church that takes down every barrier and wall that separates people. We need to remember that God looks at His family on earth as a heavenly Father, who will leave no one out who calls upon the name of His Son; nor does He prefer one over another.[4]

2. Romans 2:10-11.
3. 1 John 2:15-17.
4. 2 Peter 3:9; Acts 10:34-35.

The twenty-first century Church must remember what God's Word is all about, and must follow the lead of Jesus Christ fully. Then people will not be led down paths of inconsistency through an emphasis on something that isn't important to God.

2. The Church of the twenty-first century should focus on the same kind of ministries in which Jesus Christ was involved.

You don't have to be a theologian to pinpoint the focus of the ministry of Jesus Christ. He made it abundantly clear in the opening statement of His ministry in Luke 4:18. He came to preach the gospel to the poor, to the brokenhearted, to those who had been made captive, and to the oppressed. Again and again, He gave examples of disenfranchised and rejected individuals who didn't seem to fit into mainstream society. Since Jesus obviously reached out to and loved these people dearly, the Church of the twenty-first century must do the same.

Even a casual reading of the Gospels will show that Jesus Christ was very much concerned about the poor. In the story of Lazarus and the rich man, which appears in Luke 16:19-31, a rich man dined on sumptuous meals every day, while disregarding the obvious need of a poor man named Lazarus who lay at his gate. The obvious message behind this story is that righteous people do not let starving people suffer at their doors while they eat their self-indulgent meals day after day.

Jesus described another rich man who had filled his barns with his excess harvest instead of sharing his bounty with the needy around him. Then the wealthy hoarder said, "I will fill my barns and even build bigger barns and sit back and say to myself, 'Soul, take your rest.' " Jesus abruptly ended the story by saying, "But God said unto him, Thou fool, this night thy soul shall be required of thee...."[5] Since Jesus was constantly giving these kinds of accounts, isn't it obvious that He wants us to have this thrust as a part of our ministry too?

Some may wish it wasn't true, but Jesus Christ purposely crossed over racial lines to bring all people into His Kingdom. The story of the Samaritan woman in John 4:5-42 is a classic example. He not only offended the religious types of His day by speaking to a woman in public, but He

---

5. Luke 12:15-21.

specifically chose a "second-class" Samaritan woman who had a reputation as a harlot! The focus of this story was that true servants of God must be willing to minister to the needs of people—no matter how many racial, cultural, or economic lines they have to cross.

We all know the story of the "good Samaritan."[6] First of all, we should realize that the very phrase, "good Samaritan," was an oxymoron, a mix of two opposites, an impossibility in the minds of the Jews. They believed that the word *good* could never be applied to "half-breed religious heretics" like the Samaritans.

When a Jewish man fell victim to some thieves and was left to die in a roadside ditch, religious leaders of his own race and religious belief system passed him by on the other side. Jesus purposely had the good Samaritan, a man from a despised race and culture, stop by and see the need. Not only did he see the Jewish man's need, but this Samaritan pulled him from the ditch and ministered to his wounds. Then he put the wounded man on his own donkey and took him to a place where he could recover.

Here again, the Master's focus was on reaching and ministering to people who were in trouble. In fact, Jesus even defines our neighbor as being the one who needs our help.

The story of the prodigal son reveals the very heart of Jesus.[7] The Lord told the story of a man's younger son who had spent all his inheritance on harlots and wild living in a far country, then realized he needed help. Jesus made it abundantly clear that the boy's father was faithfully waiting for his lost son to return home.

This story speaks volumes about people in our day who desperately need to "come home." Even though the older son, who had stayed home with his father, was very much opposed to his younger brother returning to the family (and the family wealth), Jesus made it clear that the prodigal son was joyfully reclaimed and restored to his original position! We need to carefully reexamine some of the ministry needs of our day, including the needs of modern "lepers" with AIDS and the HIV virus, prostitutes, drug users, and others whom many people hope won't come to their house.

---

6. Luke 10:30-37.
7. Luke 15:11-32.

Even the story of Jesus ministering to lepers reveals an important focus of His concern.[8] Lepers were outcasts of society in Jesus' day; yet Jesus crossed over every obstacle to minister to their needs. Even more shocking was His determination to reach out and touch these outcasts—in spite of the customs and laws of His day. All these things clearly establish the proper focus of our ministry in the Church of the twenty-first century!

3. The Church of the twenty-first century should speak to man's original potential to be in the image of God, and not emphasize man's unworthiness and fallen nature.

The Bible's account of the creation says God made man in His image and likeness.[9] This creation and divine intention preceded the fall, and it certainly preceded the fallen condition of man in later years.[10] It was and still is God's full intention to have a creature of His own likeness with whom He can fellowship. We need to place the same emphasis on our ministry to mankind in the twenty-first century.

I do not believe we will ever reach the unsaved by constantly emphasizing their sin. We will reach them by emphasizing their God-given potential and the eternal purpose for which they were each created.

The twenty-first century Church must address again and again how man thinks, because man's thoughts are a powerful force. As the Word says, "For as [a man] thinketh in his heart, so is he."[11] We need to guard our minds. Could it be that many of our sicknesses and diseases stem from the thoughts we think?[12] If this is the case, then more and more the Church must address the thought process of man. The more a person is relieved of fear, anxiety, feelings of inadequacy, and rejection, the more he or she can focus on potential rather than on difficulty.

We are deeply indebted to men like Norman Vincent Peale and Dr. Robert Schuller. These men have emphasized the need for men and women to think in a proper direction. I have heard testimonies of many people who have been brought to a more comfortable position in life, and others who

---

8. Matthew 8:2-3; 11:5.
9. Genesis 1:26.
10. Genesis 3:6-24.
11. Proverbs 23:7a.
12. Proverbs 13:12; 17:22.

were healed, because they learned how to think properly. Although some who proclaim this message have misunderstood or misapplied its principles, and though some have even moved on into false doctrine, the biblical teaching that positive thinking is a powerful force must be preached to the Church of the twenty-first century.

It also should be pointed out that the words of our mouth are very important.[13] In fact, the Bible says the power of life and death literally rests in the tongue.[14] The more that the Church of the twenty-first century learns how to think and speak properly, the sooner we will come into the maturity required before the return of Christ.

If God spoke the universe into existence,[15] then we, as creatures created in His image, must carefully consider the creative power of our words. It seems to me that we have much to learn about the importance of our speech in relationship to our well-being.[16]

4. The Church of the twenty-first century should present Jesus Christ as the chief cornerstone without apology or compromise.[17]

Despite continual claims that we are living in a "secular society," the religions of the world seem to be growing in both number and influence upon mankind. We have learned that we can talk about "God" almost anywhere without bringing an offense. That is because the generic term, "God," can mean many things to all people. There are those who even call evil forces the "god" of their lives.

Everything changes the instant we speak the name of Jesus Christ (unless it is part of an oath). In recent times, I have been invited to attend major events for the purpose of offering an invocation or a prayer. Many times, I have received written notes from the sponsors asking that I not use the name of Jesus Christ "because it may be offensive to some people of the Islamic or Jewish religion" who would be present. We must address this issue with courage and with understanding.

---

13. Matthew 12:37.
14. Proverbs 18:21.
15. Hebrews 11:3.
16. Matthew 15:18.
17. 1 Peter 2:6-8.

The Word of God is clear and direct: It is the name of Jesus Christ that brings offense.[18] Yet, He is the only source of our salvation, for "there is none other name under heaven given among men, whereby we must be saved."[19]

The United States, more than any other country in the world, is seeing a phenomenal proliferation of religions, sects, and doctrines, along with an equally strong rise of interest in the hearts of people. This accounts for the sudden popularity of religious leaders like Louis Farrakhan. It is interesting to me that Farrakhan recently talked in the media about being an "Islamic Christian." That is like claiming light and darkness are the same. The truth is that if there is another way of salvation other than Jesus Christ, then as Christians, we do not have the right to lay claim to the Messiah.

The Scriptures say it is only through the death and resurrection of Jesus Christ our Lord that we have eternal life.[20] God has offered no other plan of reconciliation. Unfortunately, I believe we will begin to see more and more compromise in this area.

I am also convinced that in the twenty-first century, there will be a head-on confrontation between Christianity and Islam. We will also begin to see compromise in the area of Judaism and Christianity. Whether we want to admit it or not, Jesus Christ was rejected by the Jewish nation centuries ago as prophesied by the prophets of old.[21] At that point, the Messiah turned His face toward the world instead of just one nation. As long as we refuse to face this fact, we will remain immature and certainly unprepared to be the Bride for whom Christ is looking.

It seems to be a popular trend for various groups to highlight the needs of certain segments of our society and bring support and solutions by having marches and addressing problems that are supposed to be unique to that particular race. The effort is to talk about the need and their "cause," rather than the motivation behind it. It's very important for us to remember that the most important question that has ever been asked is Pilate's: "What shall I do then with Jesus which is called Christ?"[22] The question that

---

18. Acts 4:18; 5:40.
19. Acts 4:12.
20. John 3:36; Romans 10:9-10.
21. John 1:11-13.

stands before us today and will stand before us in eternity is, "What shall we do then with Jesus, which is called Christ?" To reject Him is to walk away from God's plan of salvation. The prophets of old foretold the coming of the Messiah. When we saw His star[23] and realized that God had fulfilled His promise that the seed of woman would overcome satan himself,[24] we knew that this issue is what the battle is about. All forces of hell attempt to destroy Jesus Christ and anything related to Him.[25] The Church of the twenty-first century, if it is to be the true Church of the Lord Jesus Christ, must address these issues head on with a great deal of courage.

5. The Church of the twenty-first century should take the lead in areas that bring solutions to human ills and particularly to the plight of planet Earth in terms of ecology.

Far too many times we, the Christian Church, have been so other-worldly minded that we have forgotten we have a responsibility of stewardship over the earth. The very first picture we have of mankind is in a garden. Man had an assignment to tend the garden and to cultivate it.[26] Nothing has changed in these areas. God still expects us to take care of this planet. As a matter of fact, in the Book of Revelation, He points out clearly that He will destroy the destroyer of the earth.[27] He takes great pleasure in His creation. Although we have prostituted it, it is still very close to the heart of God.

The Church ought not to wait for environmentalists to gather under the banner of ecology and try to take care of the earth. The Church should be in the forefront of these activities. Not only so, but when we see violence rampant in the land, we ought not to wait to see what the government is going to do about it. The Church is the reconciling force in society.[28] When we saw communities of violence in Atlanta that even the government was backing away from, it was our conviction to plunge in and become a

---

22. Matthew 27:22.
23. Numbers 24:17.
24. Genesis 3:15.
25. Revelation 12:4,13.
26. Genesis 2:8,15.
27. Revelation 11:18.
28. 2 Corinthians 5:18-19.

solution. Not only have we done so in Bankhead Courts, but by now in many other housing projects where drugs and violence were an everyday menu. Let it be said that the Church of the twenty-first century must be tremendously solution-oriented.[29] It must not back away with fear from any of the grave problems.

As we see wars and more wars, we must also speak out for the peace process. It is very easy for the Church to hide under the banner of nationalism and talk about national security. Be it known to everyone and particularly to the Church of the twenty-first century, that God is opposed to killing.[30] God does not give any right to kill. Even though there are those times when police force may be necessary,[31] both locally and internationally, this is not the perfect will of God. The Church should be the one to stand up in opposition to the continuing building up of armor that one day will be released to kill mankind.

Where there is hunger in the earth, it should be the Church that brings food to the hungry bodies as well as hungry spirits.[32] We have at our church what we call the ministry of "Joseph's Storehouse." This is a place where we constantly provide food and clothing for poor people. We have learned there are corporations that are willing to give goods to the Church to be properly distributed. All the Church needs to do is to be bold enough to step out and say, "There is no need to allow people to go hungry." As I have said again and again, the greatest battle in the future will be between the haves and the have-nots. It should be the Church that stands there to reach out to the wealthy and to provide food and clothing for the poor. This is the role of the Church.[33]

Wherever there is ignorance, it is the role of the Church to deal with it. The Word of the Lord makes it clear that because of ignorance, people perish.[34] If we bring enlightenment and understanding to the hearts of people, they will be lifted to a new dimension in life. The Church should be in the forefront of all programs that have to do with literacy. We should not wait

---

29. 1 Corinthians 2:9-16.
30. Exodus 20:13.
31. Romans 13:1-4.
32. Matthew 25:34-40.
33. James 2:15-16.
34. Hosea 4:6.

for the government or for public education. It is the responsibility of the Church to enlighten the minds of people. The local church of the twenty-first century must address the educational processes, not only of its own membership, but also of the community it serves.

Here again, we see Jesus addressing these particular areas. He took much time in teaching His disciples and in telling them how they should go and teach others.[35] It is important for us to realize that ignorance is not of God. God is a God of great wisdom. If we are to be in the image of God, then we must address ignorance from a new point of view. Why wait for some system of the world to move in and try to educate society[36] when this is the role of the Church, and we should be leaders in this area?

   6. The Church of the twenty-first century must address and define its
       structure and become accountable as well.

The world today stands with a big question mark in its mind as to what is the proper structure of the Church. Some turn to the Pope and to the Roman Catholic Church. Others turn to denominational definitions, whether it be Methodist, Baptist, Presbyterian, Episcopalian, Pentecostal, etc.

The problem that I have seen, particularly in some of the nations where we have churches over which I am a bishop, is that they do not understand the structure of the Church. I recently was in Venezuela addressing a press corp. Of course, the primary religion in Venezuela is the Roman Catholic Church. When they spoke to me as a bishop, they wanted to know my credibility and with whom I was associated. When I explained to them it was the International Communion of Charismatic Churches, they then opened the door for me to have communication as a bishop. I was then able to speak not only to the bishops in that area, but also to the government, because they understood the structure.

I am not suggesting that I know how to handle a proper structure for the twenty-first century. What I am saying, however, is that there ought to be enough eldership to sit down together to look at what the structure should be like. Many do not understand that the office of a bishop is an administrative office, not an office called of God. It is like a superintendent or

---

35. Matthew 28:19-20.
36. Matthew 16:6,12.

an overseer. It just so happens that the Word of God uses the term *bishop.*[37] But whatever the eldership is called, whether it be bishop, superintendent, overseer, or elder, there should be a place where men and women of maturity can sit down and say, "Here is how the structure should look."[38]

We have seen a surge of people who call themselves apostles and prophets. However, very little time is spent saying who an apostle is or what the requirements are to be a prophet. One is not an apostle or prophet simply because he calls himself one. The called-out ministries of God listed in His Word are the apostle, prophet, evangelist, pastor, and teacher.[39] Who should decide if one is, in fact, a teacher, or a pastor, or an apostle, or prophet? There is no one really willing to address these situations and the world stands in great confusion. There may be the title of an apostle on the door of a little storefront with a dozen people gathered. Or there may be the name of a bishop. Those who are set forth by the Holy Spirit are, of course, left to God Himself. But, according to the Word of the Lord, there must be fruit of these ministries.[40] What are the requirements of apostleship? The Word gives some clear-cut requirements for being an apostle.[41] A prophet, properly understood, is one who must be judged by the words that he speaks.[42] Very little accountability is attached today to these particular titles. Although I cannot tell you I have any solutions, I do say that the Church of the twenty-first century will either address these issues, or will disintegrate into such division that it will destroy itself.[43]

What about this matter of accountability? To whom are we accountable? This not only includes church leaders,[44] but also church periodicals, those who are writers, and those who are teachers in educational institutions. To whom are they accountable? Anyone who is left without being accountable to someone else or to some force, will obviously be in difficulty and will have no restraint. There must be an understanding of accountability.

37. 1 Timothy 3:1.
38. Proverbs 11:14.
39. Ephesians 4:11-13.
40. Matthew 7:15-20.
41. Romans 1:1; 1 Corinthians 9:1-2; Galatians 1:1.
42. 1 Corinthians 14:29; 1 John 4:1.
43. Luke 11:17.
44. Hebrews 13:17.

If God builds the whole universe on the principle of accountability, and says that all will be judged,[45] then certainly we must begin to address matters from the standpoint of our responsibilities. It's so very simple today for someone, particularly in the United States, just to pull out from one church and begin another without there being any accountability to anyone.

When will we begin to understand that there is eldership in our cities? Traveling ministries come and go into areas where there is eldership without any acknowledgment of those who have been there for years in service. It is obvious to me that God always has someone at the gates of a city.[46] The Church of the twenty-first century must again clearly define who is responsible in these particular areas and make them accountable for their calling or for their gift. If this does not take place, we just simply go further and further into division, strife, and competition.

7. The Church of the twenty-first century must again become a Church that prays and is endued with power from the Holy Spirit.

We have formalized our prayers to the point that we all spend our time primarily listening to someone else pray. Even when we come to church, instead of there being a time of prayer and seeking God, many times we listen to a pastor pray. Indeed, there is a place for a pastoral prayer. However, there is also a place where a congregation cries out to God in intercession and prayer. It seems to me that we have seen the Holy Spirit moving in recent days to remind us of the need to pray. But this is not to be merchandised or formalized into some organization. It is simply to remind us that the Church ought to pray. Hear again the words, "Men ought always to pray, and not to faint."[47]

I do not believe that proper prayer can be separated from the Holy Spirit. In chapter 8 of Romans, we hear the instructions that when we don't know what to pray for, that the Spirit makes intercession through us.[48] It is the Holy Spirit who knows the mind of the Father. We certainly do not

---

45. 2 Corinthians 5:10.
46. Revelation 2:1,8,12,18.
47. Luke 18:1; 1 Thessalonians 5:17.
48. Romans 8:26-27.

know His mind like the Spirit knows His mind. The Church of the twenty-first century must be so Spirit-filled that it knows not only how to pray with the natural mind and with understandable phrases, but also how to pray in the Spirit and to speak from the Spirit to God, the heavenly Father.[49]

I think it's very interesting that before Jesus Christ was born, Anna was in the temple praying night and day.[50] It is not accidental that the story of Anna, who had been widowed for many years, was fasting and praying night and day for the coming of the Messiah. Could it be that Anna had a force in bringing about the birth of Jesus Christ? When we say that Jesus was born in the fullness of time,[51] be it known that man must also become involved in intercession, seeking God, that His plan that is already formalized in Heaven will come to pass on earth.[52]

A man like Elijah, who was subject to passion like we are, could pray and seal the heavens off. He could pray again and release rain.[53] Even so, by the power of prayer, we can change government. By the power of prayer, we can stop violence. By the power of prayer, we can bring solutions to mankind that can come no other way.[54]

With Atlanta as the site for the 1996 Olympics Games, my first thought was that this great event should be preceded by prayer. The games played in July, I felt, must be preceded by a prayer conclave in June. This is to prepare the hearts of the people of the local church of which I pastor, as well as those whom we might be able to influence. For as the eyes of the world are turned upon any city, God can use situations to bring about His will. Any great move of God is preceded by prayer.

Prayer will do more to bring racial harmony than any other force. If people pray together, they do not have the feelings of estrangement. If we are talking about the family of God being one blood and being cleansed by the blood of Jesus Christ, then we must pray in that same direction. Prayer

---

49. 1 Corinthians 14:14-15.
50. Luke 2:36-37.
51. Galatians 4:4.
52. Ezekiel 22:30.
53. James 5:17-18.
54. Matthew 21:21-22.

has a way of tearing down walls and of overcoming obstacles between human beings. So the Church of the twenty-first century must be a praying church to really bring itself into the proper harmony and unity that is so desired by God.

Chapter 12

The Privileged Few

For many are called, but few are chosen (Matthew 22:14).

During the late 1950's and early 1960's, I often sensed that a peculiar destiny was attached to Martin Luther King, Jr. I can't say that I knew he would die a martyr's death, but I knew he was likely to encounter dangerous and possibly fatal physical resistance in his quest for justice in race relations.

Martin Luther King, Jr., often referred to the constant threats of violence in statements like, "You know, I'm going through a lot of risk and having a lot of threats." Yet Martin Jr. never backed away from his vision. He would always add, "I know that even if something happens to me, it is the will of God."

Did he have a "martyr's complex" as some have claimed? No, the Martin Luther King, Jr., that I knew didn't have a martyr's complex. Rather, he was sensitive to the fact that he could very well be killed for his convictions. I say that because he was always saying things like, "Whatever price we have to pay…"

There was a lot of violence in those days. I can still remember the shock that pulsed through my body when Clariece and I were nearly hit by a bullet that whipped through a window in the church office on Euclid Avenue. Whoever had fired the shot (it could have been fired by either a white or a black person—we had people on both sides of Buttermilk Bottom who were upset with our stand) wanted to keep us frightened.

Radical groups like the Ku Klux Klan rarely conducted their operations in public, except under the cover of night. They went underground with their movement when Martin Luther King, Jr., and the Civil Rights

Movement as a whole, began to gain more and more powerful public allies. The KKK sensed the tide of public opinion begin to turn against their extreme racist views. Nevertheless, they still conducted activities to keep you frightened as much as possible. There was always a threat—even if it was unspoken—if you were courageous enough to take a firm public stand against racism in those days.

I think Martin Luther King, Jr., realized that he would probably be killed or injured before he reached old age. That is what I heard in his famous "I have a dream" speech. When he reached the phrase, "I've been to the mountaintop," I think he was saying more than the carnal ear could ever hear. There were even more of these references to the heart in his lesser-known speeches, and especially in the letters he used to send us at Ebenezer Baptist when he was in prison for participating in a sit-in or something.

It may sound strange to you, but I heard Martin, Jr. as a white man. Most people heard him as a black man, but as a white man listening to him speak, I heard his spirit in a way that I don't think most white people heard him. Frankly, I was drawn to that element in him because I felt that the man had heard from God. That is why I think I heard him a little differently than many heard him. I somehow sensed that the man had a high destiny that would rock this nation—and that it was likely to cost him his life.

The verse, "For many are called, but few are chosen," from Matthew 22:14, was the final statement Jesus made about guests who were invited to the royal marriage feast. Many times we wonder just "who" those few really are. As I began praying over this matter, I realized that the privileged few are those who are not only "called" of God, but also chosen to share with Him the vicarious redemption that is needed in the world today.

The Word says some were "counted worthy to suffer shame for His name."[1] This seems to indicate that the "privileged few" are not those whom we sometimes think of—no, these are people who are called to suffer with Christ![2]

We usually think of the privileged few as being people like Abraham, who was called of God to be the father of the household of the faithful. Or

1.   Acts 5:41.
2.   Romans 8:17.

we think of David, who became Israel's mightiest king and was mightily anointed to establish the kingdom of Israel. Some may think of Esther, called out to be the queen in "such an hour" when there was a great need for her. Mary was another special case, a young woman who was called of God to bear His Son, Jesus Christ. The Bible clearly points out that these are indeed "privileged" people whom God had called, but what we don't realize is that in most cases, anyone who is "called out" by God also tends to undergo great suffering.

For example, think of what Mary, the mother of Jesus, went through in her agony over her Son.[3] Many times she pondered things in her heart, but when she saw Him hanging upon the cross, she must have identified with Him in a very unique way. She had become a part of the vicarious suffering of God to bring salvation to humankind.

Jesus said of John the Baptist, "…among those born of women there has not risen one greater than John the Baptist."[4] Look at the Bible record closely. John the Baptist was not only imprisoned in the end, but he also was beheaded.[5] Indeed he became a part of the "privileged few" who had entered into the redemptive process with Jesus Christ to bring salvation to the world.

I believe God will call many who will become great warriors in the Kingdom of God in the twenty-first century. Many of these warriors have a destiny to tear down the remaining walls of partition that have separated mankind for so long.[6] Jesus said, "Blessed are the peacemakers: for they shall be called the children of God."[7] As we come into this uncertain period, we will be traveling unchartered courses. It is extremely important to know that God has need of those who are willing to lay their all upon the altar.

As I come to the conclusion of this book, my heart cries out, "Lord, help me to be worthy, if necessary, to suffer for Your cause!"[8] The time is short and the hour is growing late, yet the Church continues to live in its infantile

3. Luke 2:34-35.
4. Matthew 11:11a NKJV.
5. Matthew 14:10.
6. Ephesians 2:14.
7. Matthew 5:9.
8. 2 Thessalonians 1:4-5.

form. We have spent so much time being taught "how to be caught up" that we have not really taken the time to mature and grow up.[9] One of God's greatest desires is for us to be His children—to live in maturity so we may minister light to those who are in darkness.

As Isaiah of old, let us return to the altar with a determination not to leave until we have a true glimpse of God as He is. It is in that moment that we will see our need for God's help, and that it is through His purging power that we are prepared to be proper servants for the Kingdom of God. Then and then alone can we say, "Lord, here am I, send me."[10]

God has a great need for men and women of courage today, for people who are willing to step out into new and untested areas. There will be innovative ways to bring God's peace to this planet, but we have to listen to the Spirit to learn His ways. We can still hear those words of prophetic power, "Peace on earth, good will toward men" ringing in our ears.[11] How will this take place?

I believe the Church of the twenty-first century must address the "building of communities" as never before. We will not build these communities to isolate ourselves from certain segments of society; rather, they will be built to bring together an "impossible" amalgamation of people as living proof that in Christ, we can live together.

In Christ there is neither bond nor free, Jew nor Gentile, male nor female, but a oneness.[12] We all are under the one banner of the Lord Jesus Christ, in whom we have become one blood and one nation. There is no need in the world today that is greater than the need to see a demonstration of how people of diverse backgrounds can live together in peace. If we are to see the return of the Lord Jesus Christ, then a witness to the Kingdom of God must arise that will challenge the entrenched systems of this world. This helps us understand why Jesus said that when the gospel of the Kingdom had been witnessed, or demonstrated, before the nations of the earth, then the Messiah would return.[13]

---

9. Ephesians 4:14-16.
10. Isaiah 6:6-8.
11. Luke 2:14.
12. Galatians 3:27-28.
13. Matthew 24:14.

How can the world look at the Church today and truly say, "We have seen a microcosmic view of the Kingdom of God," when we are so divided? If we are to live on this earth according to the Lord's directions from above, we must learn to do it in such a way that demonstrates God's love to all mankind. The ax must be laid to the root of all prejudice and bitterness between peoples. We must go back again and review God's Word to rediscover the true meaning of Pentecost!

We must see people gathered from every nation and tongue worshiping God together with a single voice. The time has come to hear the one word understood in all languages of the earth—Hallelujah!—raised in honor to the Most High God. Perhaps we should listen very carefully to the words of "The Hallelujah Chorus," that great song penned many years ago...

The Hallelujah Chorus
From *The Messiah*, by George Frederick Handel.

Hallelujah! Hallelujah! Hallelujah! Hallelujah! Hallelujah!
Hallelujah! Hallelujah! Hallelujah! Hallelujah! Hallelujah!
For the Lord God Omnipotent reigneth.
Hallelujah! Hallelujah! Hallelujah! Hallelujah!
For the Lord God Omnipotent reigneth.
Hallelujah! Hallelujah! Hallelujah! Hallelujah!
The kingdom of this world is become
the kingdom of our Lord and of His Christ, and of His Christ
And He shall reign forever and ever
King of Kings, and Lord of Lords.
King of Kings, and Lord of Lords,
and He shall reign, forever and ever, forever and ever
Hallelujah! Hallelujah!
And He shall reign forever, forever and ever,
King of Kings, and Lord of Lords,
King of Kings, and Lord of Lords,
and He shall reign forever and ever,
King of Kings, and Lord of Lords,
King of Kings, and Lord of Lords,
Hallelujah! Hallelujah! Hallelujah! Hallelujah! **Hallelujah**!

"Out of Conviction"

A SECOND STATEMENT on the SOUTH'S RACIAL CRISIS
signed by 312 Ministers of Greater Atlanta
Printed by GEORGIA COUNCIL OF CHURCHES[1]

THE SECOND STATEMENT

Three hundred and twelve Ministers and Rabbis of the Greater Atlanta area, acting as individual citizens issued a statement on November 22nd, 1958, calling for the preservation of the public school system. Sixteen different denominations are represented among the signers. The text of the statement follows:

On November 3, 1957, a statement dealing with the racial crisis in the South, and signed by eighty Atlanta ministers, was released for publication. The fact that this statement, often referred to as "The Atlanta Manifesto", received widespread publicity through the secular and religious press, radio, and television, not only in the South but across the nation and abroad, was an eloquent commentary upon the nature of the crisis in which we are involved and upon the failure of many of our leaders to confront the problems of our day in a spirit of realism.

Six principles set forth in this statement as essential to the solution of our problem may be summarized as follows:

1. Freedom of speech must at all costs be preserved.

2. As Americans and as religious leaders, we have an obligation to obey the law.

---

1. Reprinted in its entirety per the original.

---

3. The Public School System must not be destroyed.

4. Hatred and scorn for those of another race, or for those who hold a position different from our own, can never be justified.

5. Communication between responsible leaders of the races must be maintained.

6. Our difficulties cannot be solved in our own strength or in human wisdom but only through prayer and in obedience to the will of God.

The months which have elapsed since the signing of that statement have been a period of deepening danger. The events of the recent past have been such as to call for growing concern on the part of all responsible citizens. In the light of these events, we are more convinced than ever of the fundamental truth of these six principles. It is abundantly clear that they cannot be ignored with impunity.

Because of our involvement in this situation, as citizens and religious leaders, it has seemed to many Atlanta clergymen that some further statement on their part is appropriate. Out of that conviction comes this second statement. Once more we speak as individual citizens of Georgia and of the United States, having authority to represent no one other than ourselves. Once more we speak in humility and penitence. At the same time, we speak out of the deep conviction of our souls as to what is right. We believe some facts are now so clear as to throw additional light upon the problems which confront us.

I. It is clearer now than ever before that, at all costs, freedom of speech must be preserved. During the year which has past, it has not become easier to speak the truth concerning our situation. There are still forces which seek to deny freedom of thought and of expression to all who do not insist upon maintaining a rigid pattern of segregation. Economic reprisals, social ostracism, and even physical violence are constant threats to those who do not conform. Such threats strike at the very heart of democracy. As we insist upon the right of honest conviction—whether right or wrong—to be heard, we would pay tribute to the courageous individuals and groups in various walks of life who have insisted that our problem must be faced in a spirit of realism, of sanity, and of good will.

II. It is clearer now than ever before that we must obey the law. Those who insist that the decision of the Supreme Court on segregation in the public schools has no binding force do great injury to our people. The Supreme Court's interpretation of the Constitution has the effect of law in our country. It is possible for that Court to err, just as it is possible for Congress to enact bad laws. The citizens of our country have the right to work through legal processes to secure the correction of judicial errors or the repeal of undesirable legislation. They do not have the right to defy laws simply because they personally hold them to be unwise or harmful. A policy of obeying only those laws or those rulings of the Court with which we agree leads inevitably to anarchy. It is time for us to face up to the fact that, under the ruling of the Supreme Court, made in the discharge of its constitutional authority, enforced segregation in the public schools is now without support in, and contrary to, national law. At times in her history the Church has opposed civil law in the name of the claims of the higher laws of God. However, we believe that the Constitution of the United States in its provisions for human rights is in accord with Divine Law, and we must, therefore, learn to live with and under the law.

We do not believe in the wisdom of massive integration and are sincerely opposed to the amalgamation of the races. We reaffirm our conviction that the integrity of each race should be maintained on a basis of mutual esteem and free choice, rather than of force. There are some areas in which some integration in schools at this time would be possible without insurmountable difficulty, as has already been demonstrated in certain sections of the South; while there are other areas where such integration would involve needless hardship and grave danger. We have the hope that, if our leaders will offer evidence of good faith toward providing constitutional rights for all citizens, the federal government will be willing to leave the working out of details in local hands. We believe it is possible, under the ruling of the Supreme Court, for States to take reasonable steps to comply with the law of the land and at the same time give due consideration to local situations and avoid an indiscriminate desegregation of the public schools.

III. It is clearer now than ever before that the Public School System must be preserved. Many of our people have been led to believe that through some ficticious legal device we could close our public schools and still provide for public education through tax funds. Recent developments in Arkansas and Virginia serve to make it abundantly clear that any such hope is based solely upon wishful thinking. The choice which confronts us now is either the end of an enforced segregation in public schools or no public schools whatever. We are alarmed to note that many political leaders are apparently willing to offer no better solution than the closing of public schools and the destruction of public education in order to maintain what has been inappropriately described as "our sacred way of life." It is inconceivable that the South should deliberately destroy its dearly bought system of public education. The results of such action in the impoverishment of countless lives, in the loss to our section, even from a purely economic, viewpoint would be a tragedy of the first magnitude. It is not likely that the South would ever recover fully from the consequences of such action. Obviously, the closing of the public schools means a small and favored portion of our youth would be educated in private institutions, while the great majority, White and Negro, would receive no school training worthy of the name. No democratic society can tolerate that situation, nor do we believe our citizens wish to sacrifice the welfare of our youth.

In this connection we would voice an emphatic protest against any suggestion that church property be used as a means of circumventing the law of the nation. The churches and synagogues owe a tremendous debt to the State and this we believe they would gladly repay in any legitimate way possible. There are times when the educational equipment of the churches should be offered to supplement the public school buildings in providing space for our growing school population, provided that the separation of Church and State shall always be recognized and maintained in such an agreement. We concur that churches and synagogues have the right, as they have always had, to engage as they may deem wise in educational enterprise in the interest of their constituencies. We believe, however, their facilities should not be offered nor demanded as a means for defying the constituted authority of our national government.

IV. It is clearer now than ever before that hatred and scorn for those of another race, or for those who hold a position different from our own can never be justified. All hatred between races and groups within society carries with it the constant threat of violence and bloodshed, as has been evidenced by the bombing of churches, synagogues, and schools even while this statement was being prepared. Defiance of one law leads to disrespect for all law. We would call upon our political leaders scrupulously to avoid the type of inflammatory utterance which has characterized too many public pronouncements in recent months and to exert an influence for sanity, for justice, and for kindness. We believe that multitudes of voters in the South as in all America are far more prepared to respond to and support fair-minded and statesmanlike attitudes and policies in political life than these men have realized. In any event, political power is by no means so important as to justify its attainment by the sacrifice of justice, of kindness, and of truth, and by the unleashing of these emotions which threaten the very life of our people.

V. It is clearer now than ever before that communication between responsible leaders of the races must be maintained. The time of danger is also the time of opportunity. It may well be that we are passing through that darkest hour which comes just before the dawn. Never has there been greater need than now for men of good will in both races to voice their convictions, to exert their influence, and to maintain open lines of communication. We are heartened by the intelligent concern and struggle of an increasing number of groups who are facing the issue and its implications. We are likewise heartened by the constructive results which are coming from those lines of communication which do exist between the races.

VI. It is clearer now than ever before that our difficulties cannot be solved in our own strength or in human wisdom but only through prayer, obedience to God, and under His blessing. The situation which confronts us is one which calls for sincere penitence, for earnest prayer, for clear thought, and for courageous action.

———————— o ————————

Believing sincerely in the principles set forth in this statement, we therefore propose the following practical steps:

1. We appeal to our churches and synagogues to encourage and promote within their fellowship a free and intelligent discussion of the issues we confront. We believe such discussion should and would give careful consideration to the moral, spiritual, and legal aspects of the crisis we face in our beloved Southland.

2. We appeal to our community and state leaders to give their most creative thought to maintaining a sound public school plan. Such plan must be consistant with the law of the land, respect and preserve the rights of all citizens, and assure the preservation of our system of public education.

3. We request the appointment of a Citizens' Commission to preserve the harmony of our community. The public officials of our city have earned the tribute of the nation for their refusal to condone violence and their efforts to realize worthy race relations. We believe that in the future the need will be great for the support of calm, intelligent public opinion. Atlanta possesses business, civic, educational, legal, political, and religious leadership of the quality to afford this support. We therefore request that representatives of this leadership from the races involved be formed into a Citizens' Commission to advise and assist in maintaining harmony and good will among all our citizens.

Every section of our state also possesses the same able leadership. We therefore believe that the appointment of a similar Citizens' Commission by the state administration would serve to preserve harmony among the citizens of Georgia.

————————— o —————————

We call upon all citizens to unite with us in dedicating ourselves to the solution of our problems humbly, patiently, in a spirit of realism, and with God's help.

Signed by:

Ackerman, Stephen W.	Beardslee, William A.
Adams, Hugh	Beverly, Harry B.
Aiken, Paul	Berman, Paul L.
Albert, Allen D., Jr.	Bell, Wade H., Jr.
Alexander, James J.	Boggs, Wade H.
Allen, Charles	Bolton, Jack G.
Allen, L. Clyde	Booth, W.T.
Allen, Reuben T., Jr.	Boozer, Jack
Alston, Wallace M.	Bowen, Boone M.
Anderson, F.S., Jr.	Bowman, Keyes, Jr.
Anderson, Thomas	Bozeman, Jack R.
Arnold, Ernest J.	Branham, Lee
Arwood, J.C.	Brewer, E.D.C.
Baggott, J.L.	Broyles, Vernon S.
Ball, Raymond J.	Brown, Robert E.
Barnett, Albert E.	Brown, Walter E.
Barrett, W.H.	Buck, Raymond
Bassett, Hunter J.	Budd, W. Candler

Buice, Lester
Burns, Robert W.
Byrd, Ralph
Cahill, Edward A.
Calhoun, Murdock McK.
Callaway, Chaudoin, 3rd.
Campbell, E.H.
Campbell, Norton, Jr.
Cannon, William R.
Cargill, E.C.
Carpenter, Cecil W.
Carter, W.G.
Cartledge, Samuel A.
Case, Russell A.
Caudill, O.V.
Cawthon, William L.
Chafin, Harry V.
Chang, Kwai Sing
Cheek, Carl R.
Claiborne, Randolph R. Jr.
Clark, Boswell J.
Clary, G.E.
Clements, Lamar
Cobb, Sam T.
Cohen, Joseph I.
Cole, C.G., Jr.
Cole, William H.
Coleman, Edwin C.
Colhoun, E. Dudley, Jr.
Cook, Walter G.
Corder, L.W.
Cowart, Walter C.
Craig, Kenneth P.
Crowe, Walter Miller
Cuthbertson, Rufus
Davis, F. McConnell
Davis, Lewis C.

DeLozier, O.L. Jr.
Demere, Charles
deOvies, Raimundo
Derrick, C.K.
Dickson, Bonneau
Dimmock, Al
Donnell, Charles L.
Doom, James L.
Drinkard, Eugene T.
Driscoll, Edward A.
Edwards, Charles E.
Enniss, P.C., Jr.
Epstein, Harry H.
Epting, Eugene L., Jr.
Esaias, John R.
Feely, O. Floyd, Jr.
Feldman, Emanuel
Fifield, Harry A.
Fleming, James P.
Floyd, Arva
Floyd, Emmett O.
Floyd, W.R.
Ford, Austin
Ford, J.T.
Foster, John N.
Freeman, Cook W.
Fry, Thomas A., Jr.
Fuhrmann, Paul T.
Fulmer, C. Luther, Jr.
Gailey, James H.
Garber, John A.
Garber, Paul Leslie
Gardner, E. Clinton
Gary, G. Robert
Gear, F.B.
Gibson, Arthur Vann
Grant, Monroe C.

Geren, William H.
Gerkin, Charles
Goe, W. Charles
Griggs, Joseph L.
Grier, Eugene M.
Grubb, Hugh M.
Guptill, Roger S.
Guthrie, F.C., Jr.
Gutzke, Manford George
Hagood, Thomas W.
Hardman, Alfred
Harper, Marvin
Harris, Albert G., Jr.
Harris, C.L.
Harris, D.D.
Hartzopoulos, Harry
Hawkins, Ralph B.
Hazelwood, W. James
Herndon, J. Emmett
Hite, B.
Hodges, Bob
Holmes, Thomas J.
Holt, Joseph W.
Hope, Montague H.
Howell, W.I., Jr.
Huckaby, Louie F.
Huie, Wade P.
Hyde, Herbert E.
Jackson, Arthur
James, D. Trigg
Jefferson, Hugh M.
Johnson, J.T.
Johnson, James V., Jr.
Jones, Bevel
Jones, Henry H.
Jordan, C. Ray
Kellum, E. Owen, Jr.
Kilpatrick, Ebb G., Jr.

Kirkpatrick, Dow
Kline, C. Benton
Laird, Sam L.
Lance, John M.
Landiss, William
Lantz, J. Edward
Laughlin, John C.
Lawrence, J.B.
Lehman, J. Edward
Lee, Robert E.
Legerton, Fitzhugh M.
Libby, Robert M.G.
Lieberman, Alvin C.
Lightbourne, James
Lind, John Blix
Littell, Frank H.
Long, Nat G.
Lovin, Charles W.
Mallard, Cyrus S., Jr.
Mallard, William
Manley, W. Clay
Manning, Norman P., Jr.
Martin, Marcus R.
May, James W.
McClain, Roy O.
McCullough, Gordon
McDill, Thomas H.
McElyea, Homer C.
McIlhany, B.A.
McKee, Hugh
McMains, Harrison
McNeil, James H.
Meadow, G. Merrill
Middlebrooks, C.L., Jr.
Mill, Robert W.
Miller, P.D.
Milligan, Max

Minor, Harold W., Jr.
Minter, P.M.
Mitcham, Harry
Mitchell, George T.
Moore, James M., Jr.
Moore, Willard P.
Moorhead, Frank
Mossman, Sydney K.
Moulder, Wilton A.
Mounts, William C.
Murphy, W. Y.
Newton, William E.
Niager, Roy
Nolting, Fred L.
Obert, Leroy C.
Oglesby, Stuart R.
Oliver, Y.A.
Ozment, Robert
Patton, J.G., Jr.
Patty, John C.
Paulk, Earl F., Jr.
Pettway, Roy
Philips, J. Davison
Phillips, J.R.
Pierson, Marion
Prussner, Frederick C.
Pippin, George
Pritchard, Claude H.
Pugh, R. Quinn
Ray, Archie C.
Renz, Paul J.
Richards, Ellis H.
Richards, J. McDowell
Riddle, James H.
Riegel, Robert G.
Roberson, Jesse J.
Roberts, Joe A.

Robinson, William C.
Roebuck, Floyd F.
Rogers, Thomas
Roosa, William V.
Ross, Frank M.
Roper, Charles M.
Rothschild, Jacob M.
Rudisill, E.D.
Rumble, Lester
Runyon, Theodore, Jr.
Sadler, John H.
Sanders, Walter E.
Sandifer, C.L.
Saussy, Hugh, Jr.
Scarborough, C.E.
Schroeder, Victor J.
Schwab, Charles F.
Scott, E.C.
Scott, H. Allen
Sells, James W.
Shands, O. Norman
Shelnutt, D.B.
Shelnutt, Fred G.
Sheppard, H. Augustus, Jr.
Sherman, Cecil
Sisson, Rembert
Smith, Clyde E.
Smith, George H.
Smith, Harvey
Smith, Herbert H., Jr.
Smith, Homer G.
Smith, Leon
Smith, W. Arnold
Smith, W. Ches, 3rd.
Smith, W. Thomas
Sneed, Wilson W.

Snyder, Lloyd H., Jr.
Sosebee, James W.
Speers, B.C., Jr.
Stender, William H.
Stephens, John C., Jr.
Stephens, Wesley
Stokes, Mack B.
Strange, Russell L.
Strickland, W. Earl
Stuart, James G.
Stucke, Clarence H.
Suhr, Karl F.
Sullins, Walter R., Jr.
Swilly, Monroe F., Jr.
Tate, J.W.
Thompson, Cecil
Thompson, Claude H.
Thompson, Gordon
Thomson, J.G.S.S.
Tisdale, Harry
Trimble, H.B.
Turner, Herman, L.
Van Landingham, L.F.
Vaught, James B.
Verdery, E.A.
Waldrop, Glen G.
Walthall, David B.

Wardlaw, Hubert G.
Warner, Jack, Jr.
Webb, W. Guy
Weber, Theodore R.
Welden, James
Wellman, Wendell
Werner, Leslie D.
West, George A.
Westermann, Ted D.
Whitfield, William J.
Wilbanks, Oliver C.
Williams, Allison
Williamson, Ralph L.
Williamson, Thom
Wilson, Eugene T.
Wise, Tillman Newton
Wohlgemuth, Paul F.
Womack, John Lee
Wood, Milton L., Jr.
Wood, Thomas M. 3rd
Wootan, Harry P., Jr.
Wootan, Harry P., Sr.
Woodward, H. Travis
Worley, Paul
Wright, George R.
Zinser, Henry A.
Zwold, Harold D.